CRIME AND PUNISHMENT

Fyodor Dostoevsky

SPARK PUBLISHING

SPARKNOTES is a registered trademark of SparkNotes LLC

Spark Publishing
A Division of Barnes & Noble
120 Fifth Avenue
New York, NY 10011
www.sparknotes.com

ISBN-13: 978-1-4114-0366-6
ISBN-10: 1-4114-0366-5

Please submit changes or report errors to www.sparknotes.com/errors.

Printed in the United States.

10 9 8 7 6 5 4 3 2 1

CONTENTS

CONTEXT

FYODOR DOSTOEVSKY (also spelled Dostoyevsky) is renowned as one of the world's greatest novelists and literary psychologists. His works grapple with deep political, social, and religious issues while delving into the often tortured psychology of characters whose lives are shaped by these issues. Born in Moscow in 1821, the son of a doctor, he was educated first at home and then at a boarding school. His father sent him to the St. Petersburg Academy of Military Engineering, from which he graduated in 1843. But, as he had long set his sights on literature, Dostoevsky immediately resigned his position as a sublieutenant in exchange for the much less stable life of a fiction writer. His first book, *Poor Folk,* was published to critical acclaim in 1846.

In 1847, Dostoevsky became active in socialist circles, largely because of his opposition to the institution of serfdom. On April 23, 1849, he was arrested for his participation in a group that illegally printed and distributed socialist propaganda. After spending eight months in prison, he was sentenced to death for membership in the group and led, with other members of the group, to be shot. But the execution turned out to be a mere show, meant to punish the prisoners psychologically. Dostoevsky then spent four years at a labor camp in Siberia, followed by four years of military service. Raskolnikov's time in a Siberian prison, described in the Epilogue of *Crime and Punishment,* is based on Dostoevsky's own experiences at a similar prison.

During his time in prison, Dostoevsky suffered the first of many epileptic seizures. He also underwent something of a political conversion, rejecting the radical socialist positions that had led to his arrest in favor of a conservative concern for traditional values. His dismissal of leftist political thought is evident in *Crime and Punishment*. For instance, Raskolnikov's crime is motivated, in part, by his theories about society. Lebezyatnikov, whose name is derived from the Russian word for "fawning," is obsessed with the so-called new philosophies that raged through St. Petersburg during the time that Dostoevsky was writing the novel. Luzhin, a mid-level government official, is continually afraid of being "exposed" by "nihilists."

In 1857, Dostoevsky married Mariya Dmitriyevna Isayeva, who died of consumption seven years later. He spent much of the 1860s in Western Europe experiencing the culture that was slowly invading Russia and struggled with poverty, epilepsy, and an addiction to gambling. But with the 1866 publication of *Crime and Punishment,* a long, delirious trip through the psyche of a tormented murderer, his fortunes improved. The novel's popular and critical success allowed him to keep ahead, just barely, of daunting debts and the burden of supporting a number of children left in his care after the deaths of his brother and sister. In 1867, he was married a second time, to Anna Grigoryevna Snitkina, who helped him cope with his epilepsy, depression, and gambling problems, and who had served as his stenographer for his novel *The Gambler.* After *Crime and Punishment,* Dostoevsky went on to write a number of other classics of world literature. These include *The Idiot,* published in 1868, and another masterwork, *The Brothers Karamazov,* published in 1880. He died in 1881.

Dostoevsky's novels and other writings were major influences on twentieth-century literature and philosophy. Some people saw the political themes of his novels as prescient depictions of life under the Soviet regime. The existentialist movement that took shape in the middle of the twentieth century looked to him for his descriptions of human beings confronting mortality, despair, and the anxiety of choice. Writers such as Albert Camus and Jean-Paul Sartre valued Dostoevsky's writing for his profound insights into human dilemmas, which, along with his style, themes, and unforgettable characters, continue to influence writers more than a century after his death.

PLOT OVERVIEW

RODION ROMANOVICH RASKOLNIKOV, a former student, lives in a tiny garret on the top floor of a rundown apartment building in St. Petersburg. He is sickly, dressed in rags, short on money, and talks to himself, but he is also handsome, proud, and intelligent. He is contemplating committing an awful crime, but the nature of the crime is not yet clear. He goes to the apartment of an old pawnbroker, Alyona Ivanovna, to get money for a watch and to plan the crime. Afterward, he stops for a drink at a tavern, where he meets a man named Marmeladov, who, in a fit of drunkenness, has abandoned his job and proceeded on a five-day drinking binge, afraid to return home to his family. Marmeladov tells Raskolnikov about his sickly wife, Katerina Ivanovna, and his daughter, Sonya, who has been forced into prostitution to support the family. Raskolnikov walks with Marmeladov to Marmeladov's apartment, where he meets Katerina and sees firsthand the squalid conditions in which they live.

The next day, Raskolnikov receives a letter from his mother, Pulcheria Alexandrovna, informing him that his sister, Dunya, is engaged to be married to a government official named Luzhin and that they are all moving to St. Petersburg. He goes to another tavern, where he overhears a student talking about how society would be better off if the old pawnbroker Alyona Ivanovna were dead. Later, in the streets, Raskolnikov hears that the pawnbroker will be alone in her apartment the next evening. He sleeps fitfully and wakes up the next day, finds an ax, and fashions a fake item to pawn to distract the pawnbroker. That night, he goes to her apartment and kills her. While he is rummaging through her bedroom, looking for money, her sister, Lizaveta, walks in, and Raskolnikov kills her as well. He barely escapes from the apartment without being seen, then returns to his apartment and collapses on the sofa.

Waking up the next day, Raskolnikov frantically searches his clothing for traces of blood. He receives a summons from the police, but it seems to be unrelated to the murders. At the police station, he learns that his landlady is trying to collect money that he owes her. During a conversation about the murders, Raskolnikov faints, and the police begin to suspect him. Raskolnikov returns to his room, collects the goods that he stole from the pawnbroker, and buries them under a rock in an out-of-the-way courtyard. He visits his friend Razumikhin and refuses his offer of work. Returning to his apartment, Raskolnikov falls into a fitful, nightmare-ridden sleep. After four days of fever and delirium, he wakes up to find out that his housekeeper, Nastasya, and Razumikhin have been taking care of him. He learns that Zossimov, a doctor, and Zamyotov, a young police detective, have also been visiting him. They have all noticed that Raskolnikov becomes extremely uncomfortable whenever the murders of the pawnbroker and her sister are mentioned. Luzhin, Dunya's fiancé, also makes a visit. After a confrontation with Luzhin, Raskolnikov goes to a café, where he almost confesses to Zamyotov that he is the murderer. Afterward, he impulsively goes to the apartment of the pawnbroker. On his way back home, he discovers that Marmeladov has been run over by a carriage. Raskolnikov helps to carry him back to his apartment, where Marmeladov dies. At the apartment, he meets Sonya and gives the family twenty rubles that he received from his mother. Returning with Razumikhin to his own apartment, Raskolnikov faints when he discovers that his sister and mother are there waiting for him.

Raskolnikov becomes annoyed with Pulcheria Alexandrovna and Dunya and orders them out of the room. He also commands Dunya to break her engagement with Luzhin. Razumikhin, meanwhile, falls in love with Dunya. The next morning, Razumikhin tries to explain Raskolnikov's character to Dunya and Pulcheria Alexandrovna, and then the three return to Raskolnikov's apartment. There, Zossimov greets them and tells them that Raskolnikov's condition is much improved. Raskolnikov apologizes for his behavior the night before and confesses to giving all his money to the Marmeladovs. But he soon grows angry and irritable again and demands that Dunya not marry Luzhin. Dunya tells him that she is meeting with Luzhin that evening, and that although Luzhin has requested specifically that Raskolnikov not be there, she would like him to come nevertheless. Raskolnikov agrees. At that moment, Sonya enters the room, greatly embarrassed to be in the presence of Raskolnikov's family. She invites Raskolnikov to her father's funeral, and he accepts. On her way back to her apartment, Sonya is followed by a strange man, who we later learn is Svidrigailov—Dunya's lecherous former employer who is obsessively attracted to her.

Under the pretense of trying to recover a watch he pawned, Raskolnikov visits the magistrate in charge of the murder investigation,

Porfiry Petrovich, a relative of Razumikhin's. Zamyotov is at the detective's house when Raskolnikov arrives. Raskolnikov and Porfiry have a tense conversation about the murders. Raskolnikov starts to believe that Porfiry suspects him and is trying to lead him into a trap. Afterward, Raskolnikov and Razumikhin discuss the conversation, trying to figure out if Porfiry suspects him. When Raskolnikov returns to his apartment, he learns that a man had come there looking for him. When he catches up to the man in the street, the man calls him a murderer. That night Raskolnikov dreams about the pawnbroker's murder. When he wakes up, there is a stranger in the room.

The stranger is Svidrigailov. He explains that he would like Dunya to break her engagement with Luzhin, whom he esteems unworthy of her. He offers to give Dunya the enormous sum of ten thousand rubles. He also tells Raskolnikov that his late wife, Marfa Petrovna, left Dunya three thousand rubles in her will. Raskolnikov rejects Svidrigailov's offer of money and, after hearing him talk about seeing the ghost of Marfa, suspects that he is insane. After Svidrigailov leaves, Raskolnikov and Razumikhin walk to a restaurant to meet Dunya, Pulcheria Alexandrovna, and Luzhin. Razumikhin tells Raskolnikov that he is certain that the police suspect Raskolnikov. Luzhin is insulted to find that Raskolnikov, contrary to his wishes, is in attendance at the meal. They discuss Svidrigailov's arrival in the city and the money that has been offered to Dunya. Luzhin and Raskolnikov get into an argument, during the course of which Luzhin offends everyone in the room, including his fiancée and prospective mother-in-law. Dunya breaks the engagement and forces him to leave. Everyone is overjoyed at his departure. Razumikhin starts to talk about plans to go into the publishing business as a family, but Raskolnikov ruins the mood by telling them that he does not want to see them anymore. When Raskolnikov leaves the room, Razumikhin chases him down the stairs. They stop, face-to-face, and Razumikhin realizes, without a word being spoken, that Raskolnikov is guilty of the murders. He rushes back to Dunya and Pulcheria Alexandrovna to reassure them that he will help them through whatever difficulties they encounter.

Raskolnikov goes to the apartment of Sonya Marmeladov. During their conversation, he learns that Sonya was a friend of one of his victims, Lizaveta. He forces Sonya to read to him the biblical story of Lazarus, who was resurrected by Jesus. Meanwhile, Svidrigailov eavesdrops from the apartment next door.

The following morning, Raskolnikov visits Porfiry Petrovich at the police department, supposedly in order to turn in a formal request for his pawned watch. As they converse, Raskolnikov starts to feel again that Porfiry is trying to lead him into a trap. Eventually, he breaks under the pressure and accuses Porfiry of playing psychological games with him. At the height of tension between them, Nikolai, a workman who is being held under suspicion for the murders, bursts into the room and confesses to the murders. On the way to Katerina Ivanovna's memorial dinner for Marmeladov, Raskolnikov meets the mysterious man who called him a murderer and learns that the man actually knows very little about the case.

The scene shifts to the apartment of Luzhin and his roommate, Lebezyatnikov, where Luzhin is nursing his hatred for Raskolnikov, whom he blames for the breaking of his engagement to Dunya. Although Luzhin has been invited to Marmeladov's memorial dinner, he refuses to go. He invites Sonya to his room and gives her a ten-ruble bill. Katerina's memorial dinner goes poorly. The widow is extremely fussy and proud, but few guests have shown up, and, except for Raskolnikov, those that have are drunk and crude. Luzhin then enters the room and accuses Sonya of stealing a one-hundred-ruble bill. Sonya denies his claim, but the bill is discovered in one of her pockets. Just as everyone is about to label Sonya a thief, however, Lebezyatnikov enters and tells the room that he saw Luzhin slip the bill into Sonya's pocket as she was leaving his room. Raskolnikov explains that Luzhin was probably trying to embarrass him by discrediting Sonya. Luzhin leaves, and a fight breaks out between Katerina and her landlady.

After the dinner, Raskolnikov goes to Sonya's room and confesses the murders to her. They have a long conversation about his confused motives. Sonya tries to convince him to confess to the authorities. Lebezyatnikov then enters and informs them that Katerina Ivanovna seems to have gone mad—she is parading the children in the streets, begging for money. Sonya rushes out to find them while Raskolnikov goes back to his room and talks to Dunya. He soon returns to the street and sees Katerina dancing and singing wildly. She collapses after a confrontation with a policeman and, soon after being brought back to her room, dies. Svidrigailov appears and offers to pay for the funeral and the care of the children. He reveals to Raskolnikov that he knows Raskolnikov is the murderer.

Raskolnikov wanders around in a haze after his confession to Sonya and the death of Katerina. Razumikhin confronts him in his room, asking him whether he has gone mad and telling him of the pain that he has caused his mother and sister. After their conversation, Porfiry Petrovich appears and apologizes for his treatment of Raskolnikov in the police station. Nonetheless, he does not believe Nikolai's confession. He accuses Raskolnikov of the murders but admits that he does not have enough evidence to arrest him. Finally, he urges him to confess, telling him that he will receive a lighter sentence if he does so. Raskolnikov goes looking for Svidrigailov, eventually finding him in a café. Svidrigailov tells him that though he is still attracted to Dunya, he has gotten engaged to a sixteen-year-old girl. Svidrigailov parts from Raskolnikov and manages to bring Dunya to his room, where he threatens to rape her after she refuses to marry him. She fires several shots at him with a revolver and misses, but when he sees how strongly she dislikes him, he allows her to leave. He takes her revolver and wanders aimlessly around St. Petersburg. He gives three thousand rubles to Dunya, fifteen thousand rubles to the family of his fiancée, and then books a room in a hotel. He sleeps fitfully and dreams of a flood and a seductive five-year-old girl. In the morning, he kills himself.

Raskolnikov, who is visiting his mother, tells her that he will always love her and then returns to his room, where he tells Dunya that he is planning to confess. After she leaves, he goes to visit Sonya, who gives him a cross to wear. On the way to the police station, he stops in a marketplace and kisses the ground. He almost pulls back from confessing when he reaches the police station and learns of Svidrigailov's suicide. The sight of Sonya, however, convinces him to go through with it, and he confesses to one of the police officials, Ilya Petrovich.

A year and a half later, Raskolnikov is in prison in Siberia, where he has been for nine months. Sonya has moved to the town outside the prison, and she visits Raskolnikov regularly and tries to ease his burden. Because of his confession, his mental confusion surrounding the murders, and testimony about his past good deeds, he has received, instead of a death sentence, a reduced sentence of eight years of hard labor in Siberia. After Raskolnikov's arrest, his mother became delirious and died. Razumikhin and Dunya were married. For a short while, Raskolnikov remains as proud and alienated from humanity as he was before his confession, but he eventually realizes that he truly loves Sonya and expresses remorse for his crime.

Character List

Rodion Romanovich Raskolnikov ("Rodya," "Rodka")
 The protagonist of the novel. A former student,
 Raskolnikov is now destitute, living in a cramped
 garret at the top of an apartment building. The main
 drama of the novel centers on his interior conflict, first
 over whether to kill the pawnbroker and later over
 whether to confess and rejoin humanity. Raskolnikov
 is ill throughout the novel, overwhelmed by his feelings
 of alienation and self-loathing.

Sofya Semyonovna Marmeladov ("Sonya," "Sonechka")
 Raskolnikov's love and Marmeladov's daughter. Sonya
 is forced to prostitute herself to support herself and the
 rest of her family. She is meek and easily embarrassed,
 but she maintains a strong religious faith. She is
 the only person with whom Raskolnikov shares a
 meaningful relationship.

Avdotya Romanovna Raskolnikov ("Dunya," "Dunechka")
 Raskolnikov's sister. Dunya is as intelligent, proud,
 and good-looking as her brother, but she is also moral
 and compassionate. She is decisive and brave, ending
 her engagement with Luzhin when he insults her
 family and fending off Svidrigailov with gunfire.

Arkady Ivanovich Svidrigailov Dunya's depraved former
 employer. Svidrigailov appears to believe, almost until
 the end of the novel, that he can make Dunya love him.
 The death of his wife, Marfa Petrovna, has made him
 generous, but he is generally a threatening presence to
 both Dunya and Raskolnikov.

Dmitri Prokofych Razumikhin Raskolnikov's friend. A poor
 ex-student, he responds to his poverty not by taking
 from others but by working even harder. Razumikhin
 is Raskolnikov's foil, illustrating through his kindness
 and amicability the extent to which Raskolnikov has

alienated himself from society. To some extent, he even serves as Raskolnikov's replacement, stepping in to advise and protect Pulcheria Alexandrovna and Dunya. His name comes from the Russian word *razum*, which means "reason" or "intelligence."

Katerina Ivanovna Marmeladov The consumptive wife of Marmeladov. Katerina Ivanovna's serious illness gives her flushed cheeks and a persistent, bloody cough. She is very proud and repeatedly declares her aristocratic heritage.

Porfiry Petrovich The magistrate in charge of investigating the murders. Porfiry Petrovich has a shrewd understanding of criminal psychology and is exquisitely aware of Raskolnikov's mental state at every step along the way from the crime to the confession. He is Raskolnikov's primary antagonist, and, though he appears only occasionally in the novel, his presence is constantly felt.

Semyon Zakharovich Marmeladov An alcoholic public official whom Raskolnikov meets at a tavern. Marmeladov is fully aware that his drinking is ruining himself and his family, but he is unable to stop. It is unclear whether his death by falling under the wheels of a carriage was a drunken accident or intentional.

Pulcheria Alexandrovna Raskolnikov Raskolnikov's mother. Pulcheria Alexandrovna is deeply devoted to her son and willing to sacrifice everything, even her own and her daughter's happiness, so that he might be successful. Even after Raskolnikov has confessed, she is unwilling to admit to herself that her son is a murderer.

Pyotr Petrovich Luzhin Dunya's fiancé. Luzhin is stingy, narrow-minded, and self-absorbed. His deepest wish is to marry a beautiful, intelligent, but desperately poor girl like Dunya so that she will be indebted to him.

Andrei Semyonovich Lebezyatnikov Luzhin's grudging
　　　　　roommate. Lebezyatnikov is a young man who is
　　　　　convinced of the rightness of the "new philosophies"
　　　　　such as nihilism that are currently raging through St.
　　　　　Petersburg. Although he is self-centered, confused,
　　　　　and immature, he nonetheless seems to possess basic
　　　　　scruples.

Alyona Ivanovna An old, withered pawnbroker whom
　　　　　Raskolnikov kills. Raskolnikov calls Alyona Ivanovna
　　　　　a "louse" and despises her for cheating the poor out of
　　　　　their money and enslaving her own sister, Lizaveta.

Lizaveta Ivanovna Alyona Ivanovna's sister. Lizaveta is simple,
　　　　　almost "idiotic," and a virtual servant to her sister.
　　　　　Sonya later reveals to Raskolnikov that she and
　　　　　Lizaveta were friends.

Zossimov Raskolnikov's doctor and a friend of Razumikhin.
　　　　　Zossimov is a young, self-congratulating man who has
　　　　　little insight into his patient's condition. He suspects
　　　　　that Raskolnikov is mentally ill.

Nastasya Petrovna ("Nastenka," "Nastasyushka") A servant
　　　　　in the house where Raskolnikov rents his "closet."
　　　　　Nastasya brings him tea and food when he requests it
　　　　　and helps care for him in his illness after the murders.

Ilya Petrovich ("Gunpowder") The police official whom
　　　　　Raskolnikov encounters after committing the murder
　　　　　and to whom he confesses at the end of the novel.
　　　　　Unlike Porfiry Petrovich, Ilya Petrovich is rather
　　　　　oblivious and prone to sudden bouts of temper (thus
　　　　　the nickname "Gunpowder").

Alexander Grigorievich Zamyotov A junior official in the police
　　　　　station who suspects that Raskolnikov is the killer of
　　　　　Alyona Ivanovna and Lizaveta.

Nikolai Dementiev ("Mikolka") A painter working in an empty apartment next to Alyona Ivanovna's on the day of the murders. Suspected of the murders and held in prison, Nikolai eventually makes a false confession.

Polina Mikhailovna Marmeladov ("Polya," "Polenka," "Polechka") The oldest daughter of Katerina Ivanovna from her former marriage.

ANALYSIS OF MAJOR CHARACTERS

RASKOLNIKOV

Raskolnikov is the protagonist of the novel, and the story is told almost exclusively from his point of view. His name derives from the Russian word *raskolnik*, meaning "schismatic" or "divided," which is appropriate since his most fundamental character trait is his alienation from human society. His pride and intellectualism lead him to disdain the rest of humanity as fit merely to perpetuate the species. In contrast, he believes that he is part of an elite "superman" echelon and can consequently transgress accepted moral standards for higher purposes such as utilitarian good. However, that guilt that torments him after he murders Alyona Ivanovna and Lizaveta and his recurring faintness at the mention of the murders serve as proof to him that he is not made of the same stuff as a true "superman" such as Napoleon. Though he grapples with the decision to confess for most of the novel and though he seems gradually to accept the reality of his mediocrity, he remains convinced that the murder of the pawnbroker was justified. His ultimate realization that he loves Sonya is the only force strong enough to transcend his ingrained contempt of humanity. Raskolnikov's relationships with the other characters in the novel do much to illuminate his personality and understanding of himself. Although he cares about Razumikhin, Pulcheria Alexandrovna, and Dunya, Raskolnikov is so caught up in his skeptical outlook that he is often unappreciative of their attempts to help him. He turns to Sonya as a fellow transgressor of social norms, but he fails to recognize that her sin is much different from his: while she truly sacrifices herself for the sake of others, he essentially commits his crime for his sake alone. Finally, his relationship with Svidrigailov is enigmatic. Though he despises the man for his depravity, he also seems to need something from him—perhaps validation of his own crime from a hardened malcontent.

SONYA

Sonya is quiet, timid, and easily embarrassed, but she is also extremely devout and devoted to her family. Her sacrifice of prostituting herself for the sake of her family is made even more poignant by the fact that it would not be necessary were her father able to control his drinking habit. Initially scared of the half-delirious Raskolnikov, Sonya, in her infinite capacity for understanding, begins to care deeply about him. She is not horrified by his crimes, but rather, concerned for his soul and mental well-being, urges him to confess. Raskolnikov thinks of her, at first, as a fellow transgressor, someone who has stepped over the line between morality and immorality, just as he has. But there is a crucial difference between their transgressions that Raskolnikov is unwilling to acknowledge: she sins for the sake of others, whereas he sins for no one but himself. Sonya illustrates important social and political issues that were of concern to Dostoevsky, such as the treatment of women, the effects of poverty, the importance of religious faith, and the importance of devotion to family.

DUNYA

Dunya is Raskolnikov's sister and shares many of his traits. She is intelligent, proud, beautiful, and strong-willed. But in most other ways, she is Raskolnikov's exact opposite. Whereas he is self-centered, cruel, and prone to intellectualizing, she is self-sacrificing, kind, and exhibits endless compassion. The relationship between Dunya and Raskolnikov is always based on mutual love and respect, but it swings from one extreme of emotion to the other as Raskolnikov slowly approaches the moment of confession. In many ways, Dunya is more mature than her brother: while he grows angry and dizzy confronting Luzhin, she remains confident and in control, even when she becomes just as angry. She is the strongest female character in the novel, neither as crushed by poverty nor as timid as Sonya. If there are any heroes in *Crime and Punishment,* she, along with Razumikhin, is certainly one of them, which makes their marriage at the end of the novel particularly appropriate.

Svidrigailov

Svidrigailov is one of the most enigmatic characters in *Crime and Punishment*. Dostoevsky leaves little doubt as to Svidrigailov's status as a villain. But all of Svidrigailov's crimes, except for his attempted rape of Dunya, are behind him. We witness Svidrigailov perform goods deeds, such as giving money to the family of his fiancée, to Katerina Ivanovna and her children, and to Dunya. Although he is a violent and sneaky individual, Svidrigailov possesses the ability to accept that he cannot force reality to conform to his deepest desires. In this regard, he functions as a foil to Raskolnikov, who can accept only partially the breakdown of his presumed "superman" identity. Further, whereas Raskolnikov believes unflinchingly in the utilitarian rationale for Alyona Ivanovna's murder, Svidrigailov doesn't try to contest the death of his romantic vision when Dunya rejects him. Although the painful realization that he will never have the love of someone as honest, kind, intelligent, and beautiful as she is compels him to commit suicide, he is one of the few characters in the novel to die with dignity.

THEMES, MOTIFS & SYMBOLS

THEMES

Themes are the fundamental and often universal ideas explored in a literary work.

ALIENATION FROM SOCIETY

Alienation is the primary theme of *Crime and Punishment*. At first, Raskolnikov's pride separates him from society. He sees himself as superior to all other people and so cannot relate to anyone. Within his personal philosophy, he sees other people as tools and uses them for his own ends. After committing the murders, his isolation grows because of his intense guilt and the half-delirium into which his guilt throws him. Over and over again, Raskolnikov pushes away the people who are trying to help him, including Sonya, Dunya, Pulcheria Alexandrovna, Razumikhin, and even Porfiry Petrovich, and then suffers the consequences. In the end, he finds the total alienation that he has brought upon himself intolerable. Only in the Epilogue, when he finally realizes that he loves Sonya, does Raskolnikov break through the wall of pride and self-centeredness that has separated him from society.

THE PSYCHOLOGY OF CRIME AND PUNISHMENT

The manner in which the novel addresses crime and punishment is not exactly what one would expect. The crime is committed in Part I and the punishment comes hundreds of pages later, in the Epilogue. The real focus of the novel is not on those two endpoints but on what lies between them—an in-depth exploration of the psychology of a criminal. The inner world of Raskolnikov, with all of its doubts, deliria, second-guessing, fear, and despair, is the heart of the story. Dostoevsky concerns himself not with the actual repercussions of the murder but with the way the murder forces Raskolnikov to deal with tormenting guilt. Indeed, by focusing so little on Raskolnikov's imprisonment, Dostoevsky seems to suggest that actual punishment is much less terrible than the stress and anxiety of trying to avoid punishment. Porfiry Petrovich emphasizes the psychological angle of the novel, as he shrewdly realizes that Raskolnikov is the killer and makes several speeches in which he details the workings of Raskolnikov's mind after the killing. Because he understands that a guilt-ridden criminal must necessarily experience mental torture, he is certain that Raskolnikov will eventually confess or go mad. The expert mind games that he plays with Raskolnikov strengthen the sense that the novel's outcome is inevitable because of the nature of the human psyche.

THE IDEA OF THE SUPERMAN

At the beginning of the novel, Raskolnikov sees himself as a "superman," a person who is extraordinary and thus above the moral rules that govern the rest of humanity. His vaunted estimation of himself compels him to separate himself from society. His murder of the pawnbroker is, in part, a consequence of his belief that he is above the law and an attempt to establish the truth of his superiority. Raskolnikov's inability to quell his subsequent feelings of guilt, however, proves to him that he is not a "superman." Although he realizes his failure to live up to what he has envisioned for himself, he is nevertheless unwilling to accept the total deconstruction of this identity. He continues to resist the idea that he is as mediocre as the rest of humanity by maintaining to himself that the murder was justified. It is only in his final surrender to his love for Sonya, and his realization of the joys in such surrender, that he can finally escape his conception of himself as a superman and the terrible isolation such a belief brought upon him.

NIHILISM

Nihilism was a philosophical position developed in Russia in the 1850s and 1860s, known for "negating more," in the words of Lebezyatnikov. It rejected family and societal bonds and emotional and aesthetic concerns in favor of a strict materialism, or the idea that there is no "mind" or "soul" outside of the physical world. Linked to nihilism is utilitarianism, or the idea that moral decisions should be based on the rule of the greatest happiness for the largest number of people. Raskolnikov originally justifies the murder of Alyona on utilitarian grounds, claiming that a "louse" has been removed from society. Whether or not the murder is actually a utilitarian act, Raskolnikov is certainly a nihilist; completely unsentimental for most of the novel, he cares nothing about the emotions of others. Similarly, he utterly disregards social conventions that run counter to the austere interactions that he desires with the world.

However, at the end of the novel, as Raskolnikov discovers love, he throws off his nihilism. Through this action, the novel condemns nihilism as empty.

Motifs

Motifs are recurring structures, contrasts, and literary devices that can help to develop and inform the text's major themes.

Poverty

Poverty is ubiquitous in the St. Petersburg of Dostoevsky's novel. Almost every character in the novel—except Luzhin, Svidrigailov, and the police officials—is desperately poor, including the Marmeladovs, the Raskolnikovs, Razumikhin, and various lesser characters. While poverty inherently forces families to bond together, Raskolnikov often attempts to distance himself from Pulcheria Alexandrovna and Dunya. He scolds his sister when he thinks that she is marrying to help him out financially; he also rejects Razumikhin's offer of a job. Dostoevsky's descriptions of poverty allow him to address important social issues and to create rich, problematic situations in which the only way to survive is through self-sacrifice. As a result, poverty enables characters such as Sonya and Dunya to demonstrate their strength and compassion.

Symbols

Symbols are objects, characters, figures, and colors used to represent abstract ideas or concepts.

The City

The city of St. Petersburg as represented in Dostoevsky's novel is dirty and crowded. Drunks are sprawled on the street in broad daylight, consumptive women beat their children and beg for money, and everyone is crowded into tiny, noisy apartments. The clutter and chaos of St. Petersburg is a twofold symbol. It represents the state of society, with all of its inequalities, prejudices, and deficits. But it also represents Raskolnikov's delirious, agitated state as he spirals through the novel toward the point of his confession and redemption. He can escape neither the city nor his warped mind. From the very beginning, the narrator describes the heat and "the odor" coming off the city, the crowds, and the disorder, and says they "all contributed to irritate the young man's already excited nerves." Indeed, it is only when Raskolnikov is forcefully removed from the city to a prison in a small town in Siberia that he is able to regain compassion and balance.

THE CROSS

The cross that Sonya gives to Raskolnikov before he goes to the police station to confess is an important symbol of redemption for him. Throughout Christendom, of course, the cross symbolizes Jesus' self-sacrifice for the sins of humanity. Raskolnikov denies any feeling of sin or devoutness even after he receives the cross; the cross symbolizes not that he has achieved redemption or even understood what Sonya believes religion can offer him, but that he has begun on the path toward recognition of the sins that he has committed. That Sonya is the one who gives him the cross has special significance: she gives of herself to bring him back to humanity, and her love and concern for him, like that of Jesus, according to Christianity, will ultimately save and renew him.

Summary & Analysis

Part I: Chapter I

Summary: Chapter I

A young man leaves his boardinghouse room on an uncomfortably hot summer's day in St. Petersburg. As he descends the steps, he is overcome with a dread of meeting his landlady, who lives on the floor below. He owes her several months' rent and recoils at the thought of having to make excuses to her. The narrator states that this young man "had fallen into a state of nervous depression akin to hypochondria" and so avoids contact with other people. As he leaves the boardinghouse, the young man turns his thoughts to an extreme, though unspecified, act that he is thinking about committing. He considers himself incapable of the act—if he lacks the stomach even to face his landlady, it seems impossible that he would ever go through with the deed that he now mulls. The narrator identifies the young man as the protagonist ("our hero") and describes him as tall and handsome, with "dark auburn hair and fine dark eyes."

The young man wears ridiculously tattered clothes, but he is so contemptuous of the people who live in his wretched neighborhood—which is filthy and populated with drunks, prostitutes, and tradesmen—that he feels no embarrassment about his shoddy appearance. He walks along in a trancelike state, thinking over his awful plan, again considering the idea and then dismissing it. The narrator informs us that, over the last month, the young man has grown increasingly serious about taking action, even though the idea of doing so has disturbed and troubled him. At this particular moment, he is in the middle of a "rehearsal" of the act. He arrives at the apartment house of Alyona Ivanovna, a pawnbroker. As he walks up the stairs to her apartment, he carefully observes the building and its inhabitants in connection with his plan. He introduces himself to the pawnbroker, whom he had first met a month earlier, as a student, and we learn that the young man's name is Raskolnikov. The pawnbroker is an unattractive, shabbily dressed old woman who is suspicious, crude, and has "eyes sparkling with malice."

Though the apartment's furnishings are old and ugly, Raskolnikov notices that they are immaculately clean, thanks to the hard work of the old woman's younger sister, Lizaveta. The pawnbroker treats the young man rudely, reminding him of the money that he already owes her and offering him a small, inadequate sum for a watch that he now offers her. Raskolnikov grudgingly accepts the money, remembering that his purpose is twofold, as he is both pawning the watch for much-needed money and rehearsing the crime that he may commit. He observes that the old woman keeps her money and "pledges," or pawned items, in a chest in a back room and her keys on a ring in her right pocket. Before leaving, he tells her that he will return in a few days with another pledge and asks whether Lizaveta is usually at home at that time. Once outside, Raskolnikov is physically overcome with disgust at his plan and renounces it. Filled with a sudden thirst for alcohol, he descends into a tavern for the first time in his life and sits in a dark corner. After drinking a beer, he feels much better and again scoffs at his plan.

Analysis: Chapter I

The opening chapter of *Crime and Punishment* illuminates aspects of Raskolnikov's character that prove central to the novel. He is extremely proud, contemptuous, emotionally detached from the rest of humanity, and is in a complex, semidelirious mental state. Why he has developed this troubling mix of qualities remains an important question throughout the novel. A few clues are given at the outset: Raskolnikov is tall and handsome, which may foster his pride, while his squalid surroundings—the neighborhood in which Raskolnikov and the pawnbroker live is described in vivid terms that convey the chaos and filthiness of poor, urban neighborhoods— may have helped bring about his deteriorated mental condition. The narrator describes the heat and "the odor" coming off of the city, as well as the crowds and disorder, saying that all of these factors "contributed to irritate the young man's already excited nerves." Most important, though, each quality seems to reinforce the others, and Raskolnikov seems caught in an ever-deepening spiral: his pride leads him to perceive others as inferior, his lack of human contact leads him to increasingly abstract and inhuman ideas, and his crazed ideas cause him to separate himself from society.

Chapter I also explores the character of the pawnbroker. In some respects, Alyona Ivanovna is a foil to Raskolnikov—that is, her character contrasts with his and serves to emphasize his distinct characteristics. She is old and unattractive, while he is young and handsome; she is alert and concerned with practical business matters, while he is semidelirious and deeply in debt. The only apparent similarity between the two is that they both wear worn and tattered clothes. But even this similarity, examined more closely, reveals the difference in wealth between the two, since Raskolnikov dresses in rags because of poverty whereas the pawnbroker does so out of miserliness.

The conflict in this chapter is primarily internal, as it is throughout the novel. Here, the struggle is mostly between Raskolnikov's desire to commit the crime and his revulsion at the thought of doing so. Significantly, this inner conflict is not between his hatred of the pawnbroker and a moral objection to killing but rather between his desire to kill her and his disgust at the idea of the actual, physical performance of the deed. Morality seems to play little role in his decision and does not become a strong force in his life until the very end of the novel.

Whatever degree of innocence or harmlessness is still intact in Raskolnikov's character disappears upon his symbolic entrance into the tavern. This descent into a tavern's dingy darkness—the first of his life—parallels his descent into the seamy realm of discontent and malice. Though he already seems somewhat disturbed and though the beer seems to calm him, Raskolnikov has now crossed a figurative threshold into the muddled, violent mindset that alcohol induces.

In this opening chapter and throughout the novel, Dostoevsky withholds information to create suspense. He even delays informing us of the protagonist's name until several pages into the work, when it comes up naturally in the course of the plot. Dostoevsky informs us on the first page that the young man is contemplating some sort of "desperate deed," but he doesn't tell us what this deed is. Instead, we are given clues as the chapter progresses—for instance, that it will involve the pawnbroker and take place in her apartment. This slow revelation of detail helps to pique the reader's interest, creating suspense that adds momentum to the plot and increases the emotional impact of each event or revelation as it occurs.

PART I: CHAPTERS II–IV

SUMMARY: CHAPTER II

Inside the tavern, Raskolnikov meets a drunk man who looks like a retired government official. The man's physical appearance has obviously suffered as a result of his habitual drinking. Although his clothes are tattered, he manages to convey an air of dignity and education. Despite the jeers of the tavern's patrons and staff, the man proceeds to tell his life story to Raskolnikov. He is a self-professed drunkard married to a proud woman of noble background, Katerina Ivanovna. She married him out of desperation after a bad first marriage that resulted in three children and her disinheritance. The man, whose name is Marmeladov, has a daughter of his own, named Sonya, who has been forced to prostitute herself to support her family. Recently, Marmeladov managed to regain a job in the civil service, raising the hopes of his wife, but he lost the job in a fit of drunkenness and has not dared return home for five days. Throughout his story, Marmeladov alternates between self-reproach and justification of his behavior. He leaves the tavern for his home, taking Raskolnikov with him. The nearby Marmeladov household is a scene of misery. Though no older than thirty, Katerina is sickly and agitated. Upon seeing Marmeladov, she grabs him by the hair and loudly criticizes him. Other tenants arrive to mock the family squabble, and the landlady orders Katerina to move out. As Raskolnikov departs, he leaves the family a small amount of money, something he promptly regrets doing. He holds the Marmeladovs in disdain, especially for forcing Sonya to sacrifice herself for their sake.

SUMMARY: CHAPTER III

The next morning, Raskolnikov, in his room, is awakened by the maid, Nastasya, who brings him tea and soup and a letter from his mother, Pulcheria Alexandrovna. Nastasya tells him that the landlady wants to evict him for not paying rent. In the letter, his mother relates the experience of his sister, Dunya, as a maid. Dunya was trying to earn money to help support Raskolnikov but her employer, Svidrigailov, made improper advances toward her and her reputation in the town was nearly ruined. She has now accepted a proposal of marriage from a man named Pyotr Petrovich Luzhin, who wants to marry her because she is poor and thus will regard him as her savior. Pulcheria Alexandrovna adds that she and Dunya were not sure about the marriage at first but that Dunya agreed to it after much consideration. Both hope that Dunya's new husband will eventually be able to help Raskolnikov with his career. Mother, daughter, and fiancé will be arriving in St. Petersburg shortly. Crying, Raskolnikov finishes reading the letter and goes for a walk, talking to himself like a drunk.

SUMMARY: CHAPTER IV

On his walk, Raskolnikov decides that he will not allow the marriage to take place, as Dunya is plainly sacrificing herself to help him. Luzhin sounds stingy and disrespectful, and Raskolnikov develops a passionate hatred of him. The sight of an older man pursuing a drunk young woman interrupts his thoughts. Disgusted, he confronts the older man. A policeman shows up, and Raskolnikov explains the situation, giving the policeman some money for a cab to take the girl home. The girl goes, followed by the stranger and the policeman. Raskolnikov grows annoyed at this waste of money. The policeman, he thinks, will let the man have the girl as soon as Raskolnikov is out of sight. He suddenly realizes that he has been walking toward the home of his best friend from university, Razumikhin, whom he has not seen in four months. Razumikhin is described as warm and outgoing.

ANALYSIS: CHAPTERS II–IV

Chapter II vividly illustrates the characters of Marmeladov and his wife, Katerina Ivanovna. Each is pathetic, he in his way and she in hers, but, at the same time, each possesses an inherent sense of pride. Marmeladov is an interestingly paradoxical figure, largely because he refuses to accept responsibility for his actions even though he acknowledges that his behavior is at the root of his family's problems. Unable to escape a cycle of failure and unemployment, he goes on his drinking binge in part as a reaction to the respect and esteem that his wife gives him upon hearing of his new job. It is almost as if success of any kind is too much for him; as soon as he can, he ruins his prospects of making money and bringing the family out of its abject poverty. Nonetheless, he clings to a shred of dignity in public, and Raskolnikov can discern that he is an educated man despite his degenerate appearance. Katerina is an even more tragic figure than her husband; unlike him, she bears almost no responsibility for her condition. Her illness and bad luck in her choice of husbands has doomed her to a life of weakness and squalor. But, despite these overwhelming obstacles, her pride and dignity still remain strong.

The Marmeladovs' suffering constitutes a major subplot of the novel. Their trials and troubles are interesting in their own right, as Katerina, Marmeladov, and Sonya struggle to make ends meet and overcome daunting circumstances. Their poverty also allows Dostoevsky to include striking examples of the damaging effects of urban deprivation on quality of life. The Marmeladov subplot also intersects with the main plot at various points and illustrates aspects of Raskolnikov's character. One such point occurs at the end of Chapter II: Raskolnikov's gift of money to the Marmeladovs seems to reflect the awakening of his compassionate side. But his pride extinguishes this sentiment almost as soon as it is kindled, as he congratulates himself that "they would be in great straits tomorrow without that money of mine!" Instead of feeling pity for the family, he judges them coldly as cowards who profit willingly from Sonya's degradation and then curses himself for having given them money, which he is certain that they will waste. This pattern of acting compassionately and then pushing away the objects of his compassion repeats itself throughout the novel as Raskolnikov struggles to reconcile his haughty disdain for others with his desire to rejoin society.

Raskolnikov's pride is explored further in Chapters III and IV. The devotion of his mother and sister, who are willing to make enormous sacrifices for him, can be seen as another source of Raskolnikov's haughtiness. His reaction to Dunya's engagement further reveals his self-absorption, as he assumes that she is marrying solely for his sake and ignores the possibility that she might be marrying Luzhin to provide a better life for herself and her mother. He determines not to let her sacrifice herself for his sake, self-importantly declaring, "No, mother, it shall never be, not whilst I live. I will not have it." Whether or not Dunya herself wishes it never enters his mind.

The character of Raskolnikov's mother, Pulcheria Alexandrovna, comes through clearly in her letter. She is devoted to her son, even ready to condone her daughter's self-sacrifice for his benefit. Her letter to him serves the important role of introducing the subplot of Dunya's engagement. The letter also discusses and introduces Dunya's former employer, Svidrigailov, who becomes important to the development of the plot, and his recently deceased wife, Marfa Petrovna. Dostoevsky skillfully uses Pulcheria's letter as a device to provide these bits of context and background, so that when Raskolnikov first talks to his mother, sister, and Luzhin, we have a deeper sense of the meaning of the interaction than we would have if the characters had not already been described.

Part I: Chapters V–VII

Summary: Chapter V

Raskolnikov resolves not to meet with his old friend Razumikhin until after he has committed his awful act, if he ever does commit it. After drinking some brandy, he falls asleep in a grassy area. He dreams of an incident from his childhood in which he witnessed a group of peasants sadistically beating an old mare to death and delighting in their cruelty. In his dream, a young boy cries out against the act and nestles the dead mare's head in his arms before his father carries him away. Raskolnikov wakes stricken with horror at the act that he is contemplating and again renounces it. On a whim, he walks home through a public market, the Haymarket, where he happens to overhear Lizaveta, the pawnbroker's sister, say that she will be out of the house the next day at seven. Raskolnikov realizes that such a chance will not present itself again. He walks home terror-stricken, feeling that "all liberty of action and free-will were gone."

Summary: Chapter VI

The narrator recounts how Raskolnikov first developed the idea to kill Alyona Ivanovna (the first explicit identification of the awful deed that he is contemplating committing). Raskolnikov developed a strong hatred of her the first time he saw her. Soon after, in a bar, he overheard a conversation between a student and an officer in which the student denounced the old woman as a hateful parasite and argued that humanity would be better off if she were killed and her wealth distributed among the poor. These ideas echoed Raskolnikov's own thoughts, and he was struck by the coincidence of hearing them spoken by someone else. He became sure that it was his destiny to kill the pawnbroker.

The narrative then shifts back to the present. Raskolnikov falls into a deep sleep and doesn't wake until the following evening. Realizing it is already six o'clock, he hastily makes preparations for the crime, preparing a fake "pledge" to give to Alyona and a loop in his overcoat in which he plans to carry the ax that he will use to commit the murder. Still unsure at first, his resolve increases when he conveniently finds an ax in the caretaker's shed. He goes to Alyona's apartment, his intent to commit the crime stronger than ever. At seven-thirty, he is at Alyona's door, ringing the bell in a deliberately nonchalant manner. Someone inside unlocks the door.

SUMMARY: CHAPTER VII

The old woman lets the feverish-looking Raskolnikov in. He presents her with a fake cigarette case wrapped with a difficult knot in order to distract her. As she turns away to undo the knot, he reaches for the ax. After several blows, Alyona lies dead on the floor in a bloody heap. Raskolnikov takes her keys and goes to the back room, overcoming an urge to give up and leave. He takes a purse that had hung on her neck but is unable to find more than a few trinkets in the back room. Just then, Lizaveta enters the apartment and is paralyzed with horror at the sight of her dead sister. Raskolnikov kills her with a single blow but then realizes that the door to the apartment has been open the whole time. Terrified and desperate, he washes the blood from his hands and the ax and locks the door. Two strange men come to the door, determined to enter. When they leave for a minute, Raskolnikov manages to escape by hiding in a vacant apartment in which two painters have been working until it is safe to leave the building through the front door. Feverish, Raskolnikov takes a circuitous route home and puts the ax back where he found it before returning to his room.

ANALYSIS: CHAPTERS V–VII

In these chapters, Dostoevsky makes effective use of the literary techniques of suspense, foreshadowing, and coincidence. To build suspense, the author delays the actual commission of the crime with a dream sequence, one more renunciation of the crime, a flashback, and a description of Raskolnikov's thoughts and preparations for the crime. These postponements also reveal different aspects of Raskolnikov's character and reasoning, giving the reader a sense of his mental process as he builds up the crime. Nevertheless, much about him remains ambiguous. We still do not understand his real motives for the crime, the reasons for his poverty and isolation from society, and his surprising carelessness before and during the actual execution of the murder. Despite the elements of suspense, there is never much doubt that Raskolnikov *will* commit the crime, but the nagging question of *why* haunts the novel until, and even long after, the actual murders.

Chapter V provides a glimpse of Raskolnikov's buried capacity for compassion. His disgust at the thought of killing Alyona after he dreams of an incident from his childhood signifies his deep ambivalence about committing murder. One part of him, rational and abstract, thinks that he has every right to do it, while another part, emotional and compassionate, is repulsed by the idea. The gruesome description of the killing of the old mare in his dream also serves to foreshadow the killing of Alyona in the next chapter. The barbaric beating of the mare is described in vivid terms, heightening the emotional tone of the novel and preparing the reader for the horror of the murder. Finally, the compassionate reaction of the young Raskolnikov to the brutal act might be seen as a foreshadowing of Raskolnikov's ultimate repentance of his crime.

Coincidences abound in *Crime and Punishment*. At this point in the novel, they serve as the plot device by means of which Raskolnikov's resolve to commit the crime is made firm. His determination results from a chance discovery of a prime opportunity to commit the crime. Though Raskolnikov takes the mention of Lizaveta's impending absence as a sign that he is meant to commit the murder, it is perhaps more telling as a sign of Raskolnikov's own personality. Nothing in the world forces him to commit the crime. Instead, he searches the environment around him for excuses and opportunities that allow him to justify the horrible action that he is about to take. It is almost as though, by investing chance events with personal importance, Raskolnikov is trying to avoid his own responsibility for the crime. As coincidences that make the crime increasingly plausible accumulate, he starts to feel that he is losing control over himself and that the forces of fate are taking over. This belief in coincidences as signs of fate is tied to Raskolnikov's pride: since he believes that he is superior to other human beings, it is only natural for him to feel that circumstances should conspire to make his crime more easily accomplished. Raskolnikov is convinced, or, at least, is trying hard to *be* convinced, that he is an instrument of fate and that his actions are thus justified.

The fallacy of Raskolnikov's supposedly rational reasoning behind the crime is that his unplanned murder of Lizaveta destroys all of his justifications. Although Raskolnikov assures himself that he is committing a principled act in doing away with Alyona, the murder of her harmless sister has none of the utilitarian consequences that Raskolnikov believes the death of Alyona will have. Rather, killing Lizaveta is a selfish act that serves only to protect Raskolnikov from arrest. Committed to a path of crime from the moment he first raises the ax against Alyona, Raskolnikov unhesitatingly murders them both.

PART II: CHAPTERS I–IV

SUMMARY: CHAPTER I

> *[I]t was no longer possible for him to address these*
> *people . . . in any way at all.*
>
> *(See* QUOTATIONS, *p. 63)*

After a night of restless sleep, Raskolnikov frantically searches his clothes for traces of blood. In a pocket he discovers the pawned items that he stole and tries to hide them. He imagines that his judgment is escaping him. "Can this be the punishment already beginning? Indeed it is," he exclaims to himself. Around noon, Nastasya and the porter enter the room and hand Raskolnikov a summons to the police station. Although he is worried, Raskolnikov figures that the summons cannot be related to the murders. He proceeds to the police station, where he finds that his landlady has reported him as a debtor. He is semidelirious and argumentative. After overhearing a detective discuss the killing of the pawnbroker and her sister, Raskolnikov passes out. When he comes to, the detective, Ilya Petrovich, asks him what he was doing the previous day. Raskolnikov leaves the station deeply shaken and worried that the police suspect him of the murders.

SUMMARY: CHAPTER II

Raskolnikov returns to his room, gathers the stolen goods from the hole in the wall where he hid them, and goes for a walk. He considers dumping the items in the river but ends up burying them under a large stone in a courtyard. He walks around in an angry mood, wondering about his motives for the crime. On a whim, he visits his friend Razumikhin. The friendly Razumikhin worries about Raskolnikov's health and offers him work doing translations. Raskolnikov refuses and leaves in a huff. He wanders the streets listlessly and returns home at eight in the evening. He falls into a deep sleep, during which he dreams that the police detective is beating his landlady. He is sure it is reality and not a dream. Nastasya wakes him and brings him food the next day. She tells him that he has imagined the scene between the landlady and the detective.

SUMMARY: CHAPTER III

Raskolnikov starts to experience hallucinations and becomes extremely weak. He wakes one morning surrounded by Nastasya, his landlady, Razumikhin, and a stranger. The stranger brings Raskol-nikov thirty-five rubles from Pulcheria Alexandrovna. Raskolnikov learns that he hasn't been fully conscious in four days, and that Razumikhin, Nastasya, and the landlady have been taking care of him. Zossimov, a doctor, and Zamyotov, a detective, have also been to visit during this time. Razumikhin has managed to keep Raskol-nikov's creditors—his landlady, in particular—at bay. Razumikhin is very concerned about his friend and has brought him some new clothes, which only annoys Raskolnikov. Zossimov then enters.

Summary: Chapter IV
Zossimov, a punctilious, well-dressed man, accepts Razumikhin's invitation to a housewarming party that evening at which Zamyo-tov and others will be present. Zossimov, Razumikhin, and Nastasya discuss the murder of the pawnbroker and her sister. Razumikhin has been working to clear the name of a painter who was work-ing in the vacant apartment next to the pawnbroker's and who has been charged with the murders. Apparently, the painter was found to be in possession of some earrings that had been pawned to the old woman. Razumikhin argues that the earrings could have been dropped by the real murderer on his way out of the building and then found by the painter. As Razumikhin finishes this explanation, a strange face appears in the doorway.

Analysis: Chapters I–IV
Whereas Part I of *Crime and Punishment* was devoted to the crime, the remaining six parts of the novel are concerned with the punish-ment. At the beginning of Part II, less than a day after the crime is committed, Raskolnikov's punishment begins to unfold. As he himself notes, his punishment is to suffer emotionally and, though he would hesitate to use the word, spiritually. He becomes paranoid, worried that his senses will betray him and that he will forget some crucial detail in disposing of the stolen goods or overlook a spot of blood on his clothes. At this point, his main concern is with being caught, and he has not yet begun to worry about atoning for the crime. It is already clear that the feelings of superiority and accomplishment that he hoped would accompany the completion of the crime are nowhere to be found. Instead, he is weak, anxious, and delirious.

The main drama of the novel, the struggle between Raskolnikov's desire to confess and his desire to remain free, commences in Part II. Raskolnikov's fainting spell in the police station evidences the pressure that he feels to navigate these conflicting desires and his inability to do so. This tension and the feelings of alienation from society that Raskolnikov experiences are key elements of one of the main themes of the novel—that the individual who commits such a crime begins to feel estranged from the rest of humanity and that this suffering constitutes his true punishment.

Raskolnikov's attempt to get rid of the stolen goods, evidence of his guilt, parallels his attempt to suppress the feelings of guilt in his own mind. He opts not to dispose of the goods in the river for fear they will float to the surface, visible to all; similarly, he must stamp out any acknowledgment of guilt lest he unwittingly exhibit signs of this guilt. His burying of the goods under a heavy stone represents the smothering of his conscience.

These chapters develop the character of Razumikhin. He is a kind, caring person, willing to go out of his way to help even a surly and ungrateful friend. He is a foil to Raskolnikov—his cheerful, friendly, and relaxed manner accentuates Raskolnikov's disgruntled, antisocial, and agitated state of mind. While Raskolnikov is proudly aloof and suffers the torment brought on by his pride, Razumikhin is outgoing and seems to enjoy life. Razumikhin's accommodating qualities help to show that by engaging with humanity, one can avoid the pains of alienation from society. These qualities also help to confirm that circumstances alone do not cause Raskolnikov to commit his crime: Razumikhin, like his friend, is a poor student, but he manages to support himself without even contemplating, let alone putting into action, Raskolnikov's extreme measures.

PART II: CHAPTERS V–VII

SUMMARY: CHAPTER V

The strange man who appears in Raskolnikov's doorway introduces himself as Luzhin, Dunya's fiancé. He is pompous and affected and immediately seems to resent Razumikhin's friendly familiarity. He makes a show of interest in progressive ideas and reforms in an unsuccessful attempt to impress the younger men. Both Raskolnikov and Razumikhin treat him coldly. As Luzhin gets up to leave, Razumikhin and Zossimov return to discussing the murders. Razumikhin argues that an amateur must have committed the crime, since only a few trinkets but not the fifteen hundred rubles in the apartment were stolen. Luzhin breaks in with another attempt to make a display of his intelligence, and Razumikhin uses the opportunity to criticize his ideas. The feverish Raskolnikov then enters the conversation, denouncing Luzhin for wanting to be a benefactor to his impoverished sister. Luzhin takes great offense and storms out. Razumikhin and Zossimov are shocked at Raskolnikov's behavior. Raskolnikov angrily throws them and Nastasya out of the room. On the way out, Zossimov remarks to Razumikhin that the mere mention of the murders seems to cause Raskolnikov great irritation.

SUMMARY: CHAPTER VI
Raskolnikov, feeling suddenly clearheaded and resolute, throws on the clothes that Razumikhin bought for him and goes out. Wandering the streets, he wildly interrogates passing strangers. He enters a café, the Crystal Palace, and orders tea and a newspaper. There he meets the police inspector Zamyotov. The visibly ill Raskolnikov begins to tease the inspector about the murders and crime in general, claiming to know a great deal about both. He starts a crazed conversation in which he nearly confesses to the crime and seems to arouse Zamyotov's suspicions, but he finishes on a note that leaves Zamyotov convinced that he is merely a bit eccentric. Raskolnikov leaves hastily, bumping into Razumikhin on the stairs on his way out. They have a heated exchange, in which Razumikhin chastises his friend for going out by himself and then invites him to his party. Raskolnikov declines and walks on alone. Crossing a bridge, he is disgusted by the sight of a suicide attempt. He continues to wander and soon finds himself outside Alyona Ivanovna's home. He impulsively enters her apartment and sees two workmen redecorating it. In a daze, he asks them why the blood has been removed. He then fails to respond to their questions and is thrown out by the porter. Walking along, he notices a crowd gathered in the middle of the street.

SUMMARY: CHAPTER VII
Raskolnikov sees the drunken Marmeladov lying injured in the street, having been trampled by a horse-drawn carriage. He takes the dying man to his home nearby. There, Katerina Ivanovna tearfully tries to care for him. A doctor declares that Marmeladov is dying. Marmeladov calls for a priest, who tells Katerina to forgive, but she rejects the priest's shallow ideas, tending to her husband even as she curses him as worthless. Marmeladov dies in Sonya's arms. Raskolnikov leaves twenty rubles for the family and promises his future support. Another of Katerina's daughters, Polenka, runs after him as he leaves and asks his name on behalf of Sonya and her mother. She hugs him and he asks her to pray for him.

Full of self-satisfaction, Raskolnikov considers himself partially redeemed. He goes to visit Razumikhin, who is rather tipsy from his party. Razumikhin confides that Zossimov believes Raskolnikov to be mad, a belief reinforced by the knowledge of Raskolnikov's conversation with Zamyotov. Raskolnikov is quite faint and can barely stand up straight. Together, he and Razumikhin return to Raskolnikov's room, where they are surprised to find Pulcheria Alexandrovna and Dunya awaiting him. The two are grief-stricken, having heard of Raskolnikov's condition from Nastasya. Once inside his room, Raskolnikov collapses and Razumikhin takes charge of caring for him.

ANALYSIS: CHAPTERS V–VII

Luzhin is convincingly depicted as a pompous boor. This opinion is strengthened by the fact that the good-natured and tolerant Razumikhin, with whose sentiments the reader feels comfortable aligning him- or herself, shares it. Indeed, Dostoevsky purposely gives Luzhin an unwelcome introduction, making him appear ominously at the end of the preceding chapter. Neither his identity nor his intentions are clear. His attempts to show off his knowledge further estrange him from Raskolnikov and Razumikhin. Raskolnikov's uncontrollable pride manifests itself when he deliberately offends Luzhin; although he has good reason to dislike the man, it hardly seems appropriate for him to insult his sister's fiancé.

In Chapter VI, Raskolnikov displays an apparent desire to be found out that rivals the intensity of his desire to escape suspicion. This internal conflict becomes visible in the scene in the Crystal Palace, in which, under the influence of a wild impulse, he nearly confesses to Zamyotov. He again nearly confesses during his visit to the scene of the crime. In later chapters, Porfiry Petrovich reveals that both incidents aroused suspicion among the police. In very definite ways, Raskolnikov's impulsive and dangerous actions make him an instrument of his own downfall and his own worst enemy.

In the following chapter, Raskolnikov is shown to be capable of compassion, or at least desirous to atone for his crime, when he offers his support to the Marmeladov family. Unlike Razumikhin, who helps Raskolnikov out of nothing but kindness and a genuine sense of humanity, Raskolnikov clearly acts out of an unavoidable sense of guilt. After donating money to the Marmeladovs, he experiences "a feeling akin to that of a dead man upon suddenly receiving his pardon." Dostoevsky himself had exactly this experience, having been subjected to a mock execution after his conviction for being a member of an illegal socialist group, and he refers to it frequently in his fiction. But Raskolnikov's rebirth or resurrection does not last. He is "simply catching at a straw," according to the narrator, and it takes a much deeper repentance for him to experience peace. Nonetheless, he appears to have taken the first, minuscule step on the road to reconciliation.

Dostoevsky continues to employ the narrative device of coincidence to propel the plot forward. Here, coincidence brings Raskolnikov back into contact with the Marmeladov family, thereby uniting the main plot and a subplot, as Raskolnikov implausibly happens upon the scene just after Marmeladov is injured. This type of coincidence gives the novel a quick, almost frantic pace, as Dostoevsky forces his characters to act within the confines of the world that he has established for them.

Part III: Chapters I–III

Summary: Chapter I

Pulcheria Alexandrovna and Dunya are grief-stricken at Raskolnikov's condition, but he becomes annoyed with them and orders them out. He upsets them both by commanding Dunya to break off her engagement. Razumikhin promises to abandon his party and stay the night with Raskolnikov. Speaking to them on the stairs, the half-drunk Razumikhin tries to convince Dunya and Pulcheria Alexandrovna to leave Raskolnikov alone, offering to bring Zossimov to look after him. At first, Razumikhin frightens them with his intensity, but they soon both trust him. He, in turn, appears to be strongly attracted to Dunya. He makes drunken declarations of loyalty to her and says that Luzhin is unworthy of her. The mother and daughter return to their lodgings. The narrator describes Razumikhin's attraction to Dunya, explaining that she is beautiful, self-confident, strong, and tender, and, as if that weren't enough, Razumikhin is also somewhat drunk. After checking up on Raskolnikov, Razumikhin visits the two women, first by himself, then accompanied by Zossimov, who is thrilled to calm their fears. He remarks, however, that he believes Raskolnikov to be suffering from some sort of obsession. Outside, Razumikhin becomes violently jealous when the doctor idly compliments Dunya, and he tries to fix the doctor up with Raskolnikov's landlady instead.

SUMMARY: CHAPTER II

> *At times, however, he's . . . just inhumanly cold and*
> *callous, as if there really were two opposite characters*
> *in him.*
>
> (See QUOTATIONS, p. 64)

The next morning, Razumikhin rises from bed overcome with regret at the bold things that he said the previous night. He renounces his desire for Dunya as absurd. Still, he washes and dresses himself with extra care in preparation for his next visit with Dunya and Pulcheria Alexandrovna. He finds them quite glad to see him. He relates how Raskolnikov is doing, emphasizing his self-involvement and even cruelty. He remains calm for most of the conversation but cannot help letting his feelings for Dunya slip out again. They show him a worrisome letter from Luzhin in which Luzhin asks not to see Raskolnikov again. Luzhin also tells them that Raskolnikov donated a large portion of the money that they sent him to Marmeladov's family. Razumikhin advises Pulcheria Alexandrovna to follow her daughter's wishes in the matter. Dunya thinks Raskolnikov should meet with her fiancé despite Luzhin's request. Pulcheria Alexandrovna declares her trust in Razumikhin, to his delight. The three then go to Raskolnikov's room.

SUMMARY: CHAPTER III

Zossimov greets mother, daughter, and friend and informs them that Raskolnikov's condition has greatly improved. Raskolnikov pretends to be in a better mood and apologizes profusely to Zossimov and Razumikhin for his ingratitude. He apologizes to Pulcheria Alexandrovna for his thoughtlessness and warmly extends his hand to Dunya, a gesture that touches everyone in the room. Raskolnikov confesses to having given the money that he received from Pulcheria Alexandrovna to the Marmeladovs, and she forgives him. But the tranquillity of the scene is soon ruined when Raskolnikov becomes anxious and annoyed again. He commands Dunya not to marry Luzhin, saying that the engagement is dirty and "sordid." She retorts that she is doing nothing wrong, stating, for emphasis, that she is "guilty of no one's death." At this remark, Raskolnikov faints but recovers quickly. His sister explains to him her plan for testing her fiancé, showing him Luzhin's letter, and adding that she plans to defy his request that Raskolnikov not meet with them that evening.

Luzhin's response to the situation, she declares, will reveal his true feelings for her. Raskolnikov agrees to meet with them that night.

ANALYSIS: CHAPTERS I–III

Razumikhin's falling in love with Dunya complicates the subplot of her engagement to Luzhin. His attachment comes about with almost incredible suddenness, as he becomes infatuated with her almost as soon as he meets her. This development can be explained plausibly by Razumikhin's honesty and straightforwardness, Dunya's undeniable charms, and Razumikhin's state of drunkenness when he first meets her. Besides illustrating Razumikhin's character and advancing the plot, his mad declarations of loyalty and burning affection provide a break in the heavy tone of the novel, which has been dominated so far by descriptions of Raskolnikov's delirious downward spiral and the suffering of the Marmeladovs. In fact, the subplot of Dunya's engagement constitutes one of the few bright spots in an otherwise overwhelmingly gloomy narrative.

With the character of Zossimov, the novel takes another short break from its seriousness to inject a bit of dry humor. Zossimov, while certainly not a boor like Luzhin, has a high opinion of himself and is not afraid to show it: "the doctor retired delighted with his call, and still more with himself." But Zossimov is a minor character in the novel, and the fact that he is a doctor has little effect beyond impressing Pulcheria Alexandrovna and Dunya. Perhaps his most important contribution is his suspicion that Raskolnikov is mentally ill. That others perceive Raskolnikov's guilty conscience as mental illness may be a comment on the connection between a criminal mindset and madness, or on the inability of the medical profession to tell the difference between the two.

Dostoevsky develops Dunya thoroughly in these chapters. He shows her to be intelligent, thoughtful, and practical. Her plan for testing her fiancé and her willingness to leave herself stranded in St. Petersburg if he doesn't measure up show that she is much stronger and more resourceful than Raskolnikov believes her to be. Dunya, in fact, faces the same problems that Raskolnikov does, but she confronts them with dignity and pride. It is interesting to note that, in Raskolnikov's behavior toward Dunya, Dostoevsky reverses the conventional gender roles in nineteenth-century fiction: Dunya, a woman, proves the model of collected rationality and practicality, while Raskolnikov, a man, is lost in abstractions and prone to fainting.

Raskolnikov continues to demonstrate his complete self-absorption as the anxiety that his guilt produces gnaws at his ability to maintain his composure. His thoughtless treatment of his mother and sister, whom he has not seen in three years and whom he knows dote on him, reflects his insensitivity. Razumikhin's frank evaluation of his friend's personality reinforces this impression of Raskolnikov's misanthropy. Additionally, Raskolnikov's inner turmoil comes closer to the surface in these chapters. Zossimov's recognition of Raskolnikov's recent obsessiveness demonstrates that Raskolnikov's agitation is becoming increasingly visible, even to strangers such as the doctor. Raskolnikov's fainting spell when his sister makes a remark about not having killed anyone is another sign that he lacks the self-control needed to avoid giving himself away. In the aftermath of a crime committed according to the dictates of his intellect, his emotions are finally starting to take control.

PART III: CHAPTERS IV–VI

SUMMARY: CHAPTER IV

Sonya timidly enters Raskolnikov's room, interrupting the conversation among Raskolnikov, Pulcheria Alexandrovna, Dunya, and Razumikhin. She bashfully invites Raskolnikov to Marmeladov's funeral and the memorial dinner that Katerina has planned to follow it. She is astonished at Raskolnikov's apparent poverty. Dunya and Pulcheria Alexandrovna politely leave. Raskolnikov tells Razumikhin that he had pawned a valuable watch to Alyona Ivanovna and would like it back. He asks Razumikhin if he should speak to Porfiry Petrovich, the magistrate in charge of the case and a relative of Razumikhin's, about the missing items. Razumikhin replies that he should. Raskolnikov agrees to go visit the Marmeladovs the next day, and all three leave. As Sonya walks back to her room, a strange, middle-aged man (Svidrigailov) follows her; it turns out that he lives in the room next to hers. Meanwhile, Razumikhin and Raskolnikov go to Porfiry Petrovich's house. Along the way, Raskolnikov teases Razumikhin about his attraction to Dunya, laughing loudly and trying to appear at ease. He secretly wonders whether Porfiry has heard of his visit the previous day to the scene of the crime and contemplates confessing.

SUMMARY & ANALYSIS

Summary: Chapter V

Razumikhin is somewhat embarrassed by Raskolnikov, who bursts out laughing at him as they enter Porfiry's house. Raskolnikov tries to appear calm and confident before Porfiry, but the forced laughter comes off strangely. He becomes even more uneasy when he notices Zamyotov's presence. Razumikhin then makes things even worse by mentioning Raskolnikov's obvious distress at the mere mention of the murder case. Raskolnikov imagines that Porfiry is suspicious of him and nearly loses his cool when Porfiry mentions that Raskolnikov was the only one of the pawnbroker's clients not to come for his things immediately after the murder. Raskolnikov becomes very excited discussing his delirious wanderings of the night before. He starts to feel as though Porfiry is playing games with him. The men enter a discussion on crime, and Porfiry mentions an article that Raskolnikov had written, "On Crime," which, unbeknownst to Raskolnikov, had been published two months earlier. In the article, he argued that certain men were above the general run of humanity, and, as such, they have a right to commit murder. Porfiry coaxes Raskolnikov into elaborating on this thesis. Razumikhin finds it difficult to believe that his friend holds such a view. Just before Raskolnikov leaves, Porfiry asks him if he saw any painters at work in the building on his last visit to Alyona's, two days before the crime. Raskolnikov recognizes the trap, recalling that there were painters there on the day of the murder but not two days before, and says no.

Summary: Chapter VI

> *The old woman was a mistake perhaps, but . . . it*
> *wasn't a human being I killed, it was a principle!*
> *(See* QUOTATIONS, *p. 65)*

Razumikhin argues with Raskolnikov about whether or not the police suspect him of the murders. Raskolnikov believes that they do; Razumikhin counters that if they did suspect him, they would never have engaged him so openly in a discussion of crime. But Razumikhin eventually admits that he, too, got the impression that the police suspected Raskolnikov. The two try to analyze Porfiry Petrovich's methods, arguing over whether his final question was a trap. Raskolnikov declares that it was and that he escaped it with his answer. The two reach Raskolnikov's house, where the porter tells them that a man has just been inquiring after Raskolnikov.

Raskolnikov overtakes the man in the street. "Murderer," the man calls to him, giving him a cold look but no further explanation. Raskolnikov returns to his room and feverishly wonders about the stranger's accusation and Porfiry's suspicions. He tries to convince himself that Alyona's life was worthless. Yet he also questions his own motives for the crime and whether he actually is the sort of extraordinary "superman" that he had written about in his article. That night, he has a nightmare in which he tries to murder the pawnbroker; instead of dying, however, she laughs. He wakes to find a stranger in his room.

ANALYSIS: CHAPTERS IV–VI

In these chapters, Raskolnikov's interior conflict intensifies. He is faced with the dual task of avoiding the suspicion of Porfiry Petrovich and dealing with his own emotional turmoil. His difficulty in controlling himself at Porfiry's home and his strange dream at the end of Part III demonstrate that he is just barely avoiding a complete breakdown. The ongoing struggle between his desire to avoid suspicion and his compulsion to confess leads him to act erratically, sometimes trying to appear healthy and innocent and other times boldly risking discovery.

Raskolnikov's article "On Crime" clues the reader in to some of the rationale for committing the murder. Introducing the theme of Raskolnikov's idea of a "superman," the article argues that certain extraordinary people are above the masses of humanity and so have the right to violate moral codes, for instance, by committing murder. Razumikhin's strongly moral character reveals itself in his immediate rejection of this notion. Porfiry Petrovich, however, takes great interest in the idea—not because he agrees with it, but because he sees it as a piece of psychological evidence pointing to Raskolnikov's guilt. The discussion takes place on an intellectual plane, but the fact that Raskolnikov has actually followed through with his idea and that Porfiry suspects him of it lends the otherwise abstract discussion a tense immediacy. The conversation serves to illustrate the enormous gap between talking about violating moral boundaries and actually doing so. Interestingly, Raskolnikov's inner turmoil belies the superiority and righteousness with which his ideal "superman" is supposed to commit crimes.

The ideas that Raskolnikov expresses in his article have strong ties to nihilism, a philosophical position developed in Russia in the 1850s and 1860s. Nihilism rejected the traditional bonds of family and society as well as emotional and aesthetic concerns in favor of a strict materialism promoting the idea that there is no mind or soul outside of the physical world. A central tenet of nihilism was utilitarianism—the idea that actions are moral insofar as they work toward the greatest possible happiness for the largest number of people. As is made clear in this section, Raskolnikov's justifications for murdering Alyona are strongly utilitarian and nihilist.

Raskolnikov's nightmare reflects not so much his feelings of guilt as his fear that he doesn't actually measure up to his theoretical "superman"—and that his actions, therefore, have no justification. Even before Raskolnikov has his nightmare, the stranger's simple, direct labeling of him as "[m]urderer" makes the grandiose identity that he had created for himself begin to crumble. The defense that he mounts against this deconstruction of his assumed identity constitutes a counterattack on the debased identity that the stranger has imposed on him. In devaluing Alyona's life, Raskolnikov seeks to mitigate the criminality of the murder by emphasizing his own worth and her worthlessness. In his nightmare, however, he cannot pretend that he acted as a "superman" in killing Alyona. Indeed, the nightmare forces him to confront his mediocrity; that Alyona laughs at him when he tries to kill her reveals to him his impotency and inadequacy.

The suspense mounts in these chapters, especially with the introduction of the strange man who follows Sonya in Chapter IV and then appears in Raskolnikov's doorway at the end of Chapter VI. The more strangers that enter Raskolnikov's life, the more complicated his situation gets. Each time he pushes them away, he is, in part, trying to keep himself separate from the humanity that he disdains and maintain the abstract, lonely position from which he originally formulates his plan of killing Alyona. The entrance into the drama of the stranger, who we later find out is Svidrigailov, threatens Raskolnikov's sense of his role and thrusts him one step closer toward reengagement with society, whether he likes it or not.

PART IV: CHAPTERS I–III

SUMMARY: CHAPTER I

Svidrigailov explains that he has come to ask Raskolnikov's help in his pursuit of Dunya. Raskolnikov immediately refuses. Svidrigailov contends that he has only the purest feelings for Dunya and that, contrary to rumor, he had nothing to do with the recent death of his wife, Marfa Petrovna. He argues that he is not a monster, only a slave to passion. He then tells a story about how he came to marry his wife, saying that she took advantage of a predicament that he was in to control and dominate him. He claims to have been visited by the ghost of his dead wife several times. Raskolnikov wonders whether his visitor is insane. Svidrigailov says that he has heard of Dunya's engagement to Luzhin, who is a relative of his, and offers to help break off this inappropriate match. Svidrigailov claims that, though he once obsessed over Dunya, he is no longer in love with her but cannot bear her taking such an unsuitable husband. He wants to give her ten thousand rubles as an apology before he either marries or goes on a journey. Raskolnikov assures him that his sister will refuse the gift. Svidrigailov also tells him that his wife has left Dunya three thousand rubles in her will. He leaves, passing Razumikhin on his way out.

SUMMARY: CHAPTER II

Razumikhin and Raskolnikov walk to a restaurant. Razumikhin says that he has spoken with Porfiry Petrovich and Zamyotov and discovered that they suspect Raskolnikov of the murders, which Razumikhin finds absurd. Raskolnikov privately wonders what his friend will think when he finds out that Raskolnikov is indeed guilty. They meet with Luzhin, Dunya, and Pulcheria Alexandrovna and seat themselves around a table. Luzhin's pride is wounded by the presence of the two young men, whose absence he had specifically requested, and he resolves to punish the women. He upsets them by breaking the news of Svidrigailov's arrival in St. Petersburg. He goes on to describe the crimes and depravities that he has heard attributed to Svidrigailov, but Dunya rejects his stories as baseless gossip. Raskolnikov abruptly informs the party of his meeting with Svidrigailov and the money that was willed to Dunya by Marfa Petrovna. He refuses to say what Svidrigailov wants with Dunya. Dunya then confronts Luzhin about his annoyance at her brother's presence, and Luzhin manages to offend everyone in the room with his response. There is an angry confrontation between mother, daughter, and son on one side and fiancé on the other. Dunya orders Luzhin to leave. He does so only after insulting them. As he leaves, he blames his loss of Dunya on Raskolnikov, for whom he now harbors a deep hatred. He convinces himself that he may still have a chance with Dunya.

Summary: Chapter III

After Luzhin departs, the group is overjoyed. Razumikhin is the happiest of all. Raskolnikov, however, quickly becomes anxious again. He tells them about Svidrigailov offering to give Dunya ten thousand rubles, which both women refuse. Razumikhin offers to guard Dunya from the man, and Dunya consents. He suggests that Dunya and her mother stay on in St. Petersburg and proposes that they all go into the publishing business together. Dunya is thrilled with this idea and Raskolnikov assents as well. But then Raskolnikov abruptly gets up to leave. He states that he has resolved to separate himself from them for a long time and that they must not pursue him. The rest of the group is dismayed. Razumikhin chases after him, but Raskolnikov sends him back, telling his friend to stay with Pulcheria Alexandrovna and Dunya. The two stare at each other, and Razumikhin realizes that Raskolnikov is the murderer. He returns to the table.

Analysis: Chapters I–III

Svidrigailov is depicted as a morally weak man who doesn't seem to understand when he is unwelcome or perhaps simply doesn't care. But, unlike most of the other characters, such as the kind and compassionate Razumikhin or the miserly Alyona Ivanovna, Svidrigailov is not drawn quickly and decisively. His mental state, motives, and true nature remain enigmatic throughout the novel. Svidrigailov's entrance into the plot is almost identical to that of Luzhin: like Luzhin in Part II, Chapter IV, Svidrigailov appears unexpectedly in Raskolnikov's room, his entrance made ominous by the fact that he, a stranger, hovers over Raskolnikov at the close of the preceding chapter. Additionally, both discuss their interest in Dunya with Raskolnikov. One subtle difference between these two encounters is that Razumikhin is not present when Svidrigailov shows up; rather, Raskolnikov is alone in his room. Svidrigailov is an unreal shadow of Raskolnikov, a figment of his imagination, delusional like he is and equally dysfunctional in society.

Luzhin returns to cause mischief later in the narrative, but it is clear that his engagement with Dunya is permanently broken. In her decision to reject Luzhin, Dunya is revealed as an intelligent, confident, and decisive woman who, though willing to make sacrifices for the sake of her family, is unwilling to disgrace herself by marrying a man as crude as Luzhin. Her pride is as strong as Raskolnikov's, but, unlike his, it is laced with dignity and motivates her to maintain her integrity in the face of such ill-conceived possibilities as her engagement to Luzhin.

The breaking of the engagement is a major event not only for Dunya but also for Raskolnikov. Raskolnikov's sudden irritation after Luzhin's departure seems, at first, abrupt, but a close look at the timing of his decision to leave reveals its significance. Only after he realizes that Razumikhin will take care of Dunya and Pulcheria Alexandrovna does Raskolnikov announce his need to separate from them. Tainted by his crime, he wishes to distance himself from them, but he is unwilling to do so until he knows that they will be cared for. This consideration marks the beginning of a change in his character. For the first time, he seems to care for others and not just for himself. While Raskolnikov's decision to leave is of a different order than Sonya's prostitution and Dunya's decision to become engaged to Luzhin, it nevertheless reflects his understanding of the importance of family. The contrast between Raskolnikov's lonely, alienated thoughts and the generous affection of Pulcheria Alexandrovna and Dunya only heightens Raskolnikov's inner turmoil and his compulsion to detach himself from his family. His departure from them makes it clear that he either intends to confess voluntarily or believes that he will soon be found out—or, perhaps, that he simply cannot face the people who love him with the secret of the murders hanging over him.

PART IV: CHAPTERS IV–VI

SUMMARY: CHAPTER IV

Raskolnikov goes to Sonya's room. She is surprised and frightened by his visit. They discuss Katerina Ivanovna, whom Sonya defends as kind, childlike, and fiercely proud, though she concedes that misfortune has more or less deranged Katerina. Sonya clearly cares immensely for her stepmother and is deeply troubled to think that she might soon die, leaving her children defenseless. Yet she clings to the belief that God will provide for the family and take care of them. Sonya reveals that she was a friend of the murdered Lizaveta. In fact, Lizaveta gave Sonya a cross and a copy of the Gospels. Raskolnikov commands Sonya to read him the story of Lazarus. Sonya manages to overcome her terror of the crazed Raskolnikov and reads, shaking as she does so. It is clear that the passage has special significance for her. Raskolnikov shares with her his resolution to separate from his family and asks her to go away with him. He thinks of her as a kindred spirit, someone who has, as a prostitute, also transgressed moral law and "destroyed a life—her very own." He tells her that she will soon know who killed Lizaveta. Meanwhile, in a vacant room next door, Svidrigailov eavesdrops on the conversation.

SUMMARY: CHAPTER V

> *[F]reedom will no longer be dear to him, he'll fall to*
> *thinking, get entangled . . . he'll worry himself to death!*
> *(See QUOTATIONS, p. 66)*

The following morning, Raskolnikov pays a visit to Porfiry Petrovich at the police station. While he waits in the lobby, he mulls over his hatred for the magistrate. Once inside Porfiry's office, Raskolnikov presents him with a written request for his pawned possessions. The two embark on a long conversation in which Raskolnikov quickly starts to feel as though he has fallen into a trap. Frustrated by the games that he thinks Porfiry is playing, he asks the magistrate to submit him to the questioning discussed the previous day. Porfiry tries to put Raskolnikov at ease and become friendly with him. He chatters away, speaking mostly nonsense, though occasionally adding an enigmatic remark. He discusses the psychological methods by which he hopes to catch the murderer. He includes observations about the "youth" and "intelligence" of his suspect that are pointed directly at Raskolnikov. Throughout Porfiry's rambling monologue, Raskolnikov, though agitated, stays quiet. But after a while, he bursts out wildly, accusing the official of suspecting him and challenging Porfiry either to accuse him outright or to let him be. Porfiry tries to calm him down. But even as he does so, he reveals that he knows of Raskolnikov's recent visit to the scene of the crime. He tries to trick Raskolnikov into admitting that he sent Razumikhin to ask Porfiry about his suspicions. Raskolnikov becomes violently upset, but then a "singular incident" occurs.

SUMMARY: CHAPTER VI

Suddenly, Nikolai, the prisoner who is under suspicion for the murders, rushes into the office and confesses to the crime. Although Porfiry does not believe the man, he takes the confession seriously. He shows Raskolnikov out. As Raskolnikov is on the stairs, Porfiry detains him to say that he will need to see him again soon for more questions. Raskolnikov goes home, where he realizes that, if Nikolai hadn't burst into Porfiry's office, he might have confessed to the murders. He decides to go to the memorial dinner for Marmeladov.

Just then, the stranger who had called him a murderer the previous day appears in the doorway. The man, who identifies himself as a tenant of the pawnbroker's building, says that he witnessed Raskolnikov's visit to the crime scene and heard him question the workers about the blood. He reveals that he knows nothing more and, having overheard his conversation with Porfiry at the police station, is now sympathetic to Raskolnikov's plight. Raskolnikov is greatly relieved and feels renewed hope that he will not be caught after all.

ANALYSIS: CHAPTERS IV–VI

Dostoevsky's inclusion of the Lazarus story provides both Raskolnikov and Sonya with a model of hope for their lives. In the Christian tradition, the raising of Lazarus from death is the most profound miracle that Jesus performed while on earth. Sonya may adapt the story to her life as a promise that a similar miracle will rectify her situation, a kind of death induced by her poverty and self-sacrifice. The story also carries deep significance for the skeptical Raskolnikov. Although he claims not to believe in the story, he is moved by it, since it no doubt resonates with his sense of total alienation from society. His death has been a death of the soul. Separated from those who love him by his own pride and his terrible secret, Raskolnikov longs for some kind of chance to start anew, to be, like Lazarus, resurrected. He is still proud, but his veneer of superiority is beginning to crack.

The Lazarus story also serves as allegorical foreshadowing, predicting Raskolnikov's return to humanity at the end of the novel. Despite his conviction that killing Alyona Ivanovna was justified, Raskolnikov already feels his guilt and alienation on a deep, almost physical level. He is eventually driven to confess, if for no other reason than to put an end to the doubt and emotional turmoil that now hound him. His ultimate confession and subsequent imprisonment lead him to some form of redemption.

Sonya's humility is much more profound than her embarrassment about being a prostitute. She is a pious Christian, believing that her fate is firmly in God's hands and trusting that he is just, as Raskolnikov observes, against all proof to the contrary. It is Sonya's faith that allows her to continue surviving and helping her family to survive. The contrast between Sonya and Raskolnikov is striking, illuminating the depth of Sonya's devotion and self-sacrifice and the shallowness of Raskolnikov's pride. Raskolnikov's attempt to compare himself to Sonya as a fellow sinner falls flat, since she has turned to prostitution only out of the need to help her family, and laments her sin, while Raskolnikov has not yet repented for the murders, the first of which is shakily predicated on utilitarian grounds and the second of which is purely self-serving. Raskolnikov's blindness to these differences shows that he is still a long way from recognizing his guilt.

The psychological conflict between Raskolnikov and Porfiry Petrovich comes to a head in Chapter V. Though Raskolnikov is rightly confident that Petrovich has no evidence of his guilt, Porfiry makes full use of Raskolnikov's unease. Raskolnikov seems almost ready to confess at the end of Chapter IV, but he steps back from the edge, and, by the end of Part IV, seems to have renewed his resolve to evade punishment. His sarcastic, prideful side returns in full force, and he pulls himself away from the people around him, criticizing himself for his "weakness." The internal conflict between his pride and his desire to confess intensifies, weaving back and forth and prolonging the suspense over the eventual outcome of the struggle.

Dostoevsky continues to employ all of his characters to masterful effect, setting up an infinite number of possible coincidences and obstacles for Raskolnikov. The revelation of Svidrigailov's eavesdropping is intended purely for the reader and clearly foreshadows that Svidrigailov will use the information that he has garnered for some sinister purpose. Additionally, Dostoevsky inserts Nikolai's dramatic confession, an unexpected but perfectly timed event for Raskolnikov's benefit that allows Dostoevsky to shift the direction of the plot. As when Raskolnikov heard someone talking about a desire to kill the pawnbroker, echoing his thoughts, Raskolnikov believes that Nikolai's confession is evidence of some master plan for him.

PART V: CHAPTERS I–IV

SUMMARY: CHAPTER I

Luzhin is in his room with Lebezyatnikov, a younger man who is his roommate. Luzhin now realizes that his engagement with Dunya is irrecoverably broken. He nurses a deep hatred for Raskolnikov, and shivers to think of the money that he lost on deposits for their newlywed home and furnishings. He fantasizes that if he had given his fiancée and her mother more presents, they would not have broken the engagement. Meanwhile, he and Lebezyatnikov have been invited to the memorial dinner that Katerina Ivanovna, who lives in the same building, is holding for Marmeladov. Lebezyatnikov is a pompous fool, though Luzhin initially thought of him as a thoughtful young man who could help him navigate the new political waves of liberalism, radicalism, and nihilism washing over Russia. Luzhin invites Sonya to his room and gives the embarrassed girl a ten-ruble note.

SUMMARY: CHAPTER II

The narrator considers Katerina Ivanovna's reasons for spending more than half of the money given to them by Raskolnikov on the memorial banquet and concludes that it is probably because of her pride. Only Raskolnikov and the lowliest of the tenants, who behave rudely, attend the affair. Katerina, who claims repeatedly to be of a "noble, if not aristocratic," family, hurls insults at her low-class guests. Meanwhile, she appears increasingly unwell, coughing up blood during the meal. She ends up fighting with her landlady while her guests egg her on. In the middle of the fight, Luzhin appears in the doorway and Katerina rushes to him.

SUMMARY: CHAPTER III

Luzhin insultingly brushes Katerina aside as she implores his protection from the landlady. Turning to Sonya, he accuses her of stealing a one-hundred-ruble note. Sonya denies the theft. Katerina becomes incensed at the insult to her stepdaughter and starts raving against Luzhin and the landlady. To prove Sonya's innocence, she defiantly turns the girl's pockets out and is shocked when a one-hundred-ruble note falls out. Luzhin magnanimously agrees not to press charges. To Luzhin's horror, however, Lebezyatnikov appears and declares that he saw Luzhin place the note in Sonya's pocket earlier. Raskolnikov then explains that Luzhin was probably trying to embarrass him about his association with Sonya. Luzhin, faced with the complete ruin of his plan, tries to extricate himself by maintaining his innocence and insulting Lebezyatnikov and Raskolnikov. After Luzhin leaves, the fight between Katerina and the landlady continues. In the end, the Marmeladovs are evicted.

SUMMARY: CHAPTER IV

Raskolnikov visits Sonya in her room. He tells her that her family has been turned out of their building but urges her not to go to help them. He confesses the murders to her. Sonya responds with immense pity and promises to support Raskolnikov and not abandon him. She is astonished when he tells her that his poverty was not the motive. Rather, he says, "I was ambitious to become another Napoleon; that was why I committed a murder." He also confesses that he feels detached from other people and believed, and perhaps still believes, in his superiority over most other people. Sonya tells him that he has been punished for turning away from God. He reiterates that self-absorption fueled his actions, that he wished to prove that he was somehow extraordinary and able to transgress the moral codes that bind ordinary people. Sonya tells him that he must confess his sins publicly for God to give him peace. At first he resists, but he soon consents. Sonya promises to come to see him in prison and support him. She gives him a pendant cross to wear, similar to the one that she wears, saying that they will both bear their crosses. Just then, Lebezyatnikov knocks at the door.

Analysis: Chapters I–IV

Luzhin's profoundly materialistic and self-serving nature is brought to the fore in this section. Obsessed with money and material objects, he blames Dunya's rejection of him on entirely material motives, thinking that once she had the inheritance from Marfa Petrovna, she and her mother no longer needed him. His plan to frame Sonya solidifies his status as one of the novel's villains. His ploy is clumsy and mean-spirited, and, although he tries to maintain his pride, it is clear that he will never regain Dunya's favor. After this scene, Luzhin disappears from the narrative, never to return again, since he has played his last cards and been beaten. Dunya is now completely free to turn her attention to Razumikhin, the man whose rightness for her has been clear from the start.

Lebezyatnikov functions as a humorous and sarcastic caricature of the pompous but stupid intellectual, a proverbial emperor with no clothes. Even as he rushes to Sonya's defense, Lebezyatnikov feels the need to make little speeches about the ethics of private charity. In depicting Lebezyatnikov as obsessed with intellectual fads and unrealistic utopias, Dostoevsky criticizes the actual intellectual currents that were sweeping Russia in the 1860s, such as nihilism, and emphasizes how much more profound, albeit equally misguided, Raskolnikov's theories are.

Katerina Ivanovna appears as a tragic figure, portrayed in vivid images of coughed-up blood and inflamed cheeks. Her pride, unlike Raskolnikov's, is deeply pathetic and intertwined with her poverty. She rails against a world that she believes has unjustly punished her. Her pride motivates her to spend too much money on Marmeladov's memorial dinner, even though, with his death, the family is certain to starve. She sees the dinner as one last chance to pretend that she truly is "noble, even aristocratic." Instead, the event proves to be only one more illustration of the impossibility of escaping the poverty that surrounds her. The subplot of the Marmeladovs' unrelenting misfortune provides the reader a broader context for Raskolnikov's struggle against a society filled with injustice, poverty, anonymity, and hopelessness.

Raskolnikov's confession to Sonya and his promise to confess to the police are major developments. At the end of this section, Raskolnikov seems finally to have started on the path to resolving the torment that he has felt since the murders. His pride has given way to the realization that he is not the "superman" that he once fantasized himself to be. Still, it is important to note that his return to humanity is not happy; he still thinks of the people around him as despicable creatures and, understanding himself as part of humanity, views himself as necessarily despicable. This realization that he is only human constitutes the first big step toward confession and redemption. Though true remorse stands a long way off, the simple act of confessing to Sonya and receiving her sympathy—his first meaningful connection with another person—helps him break through his alienation from all of humanity.

These developments occur in tandem with a shift for Raskolnikov from a theoretical to a realistic understanding of matters. Whereas he initially justifies the murder of Alyona Ivanovna on the nihilist grounds of ridding humanity of a parasite, he now admits that his actions were based less in philosophy than in emotional insecurity: "All I wanted was to do some daring thing, Sonya; that was my sole motive!" By committing an exceptional act, by stepping over the normal bounds of human behavior, he had hoped to prove that he himself was exceptional. The self-serving nature of his actions, however, contradicts and undermines the utilitarian and nihilist motives that he originally professes.

PART V: CHAPTER V

In some editions, the fifth chapter of Part V is set as a chapter-long Part VI. In such editions, CRIME AND PUNISHMENT is divided into seven parts plus an epilogue, rather than the six parts plus an epilogue into which this SparkNote divides the text.

SUMMARY: CHAPTER V

Lebezyatnikov informs Sonya that Katerina Ivanovna has apparently gone mad. Katerina has visited the homes of well-to-do people, demanding their assistance, and has been violently thrown out. She has now resolved to become an organ-grinder, is tearing up her children's clothes, and has sent her children to dance in the street and beg for charity. She hopes to perform in front of one of the houses from which she was turned out to shame its inhabitants and the public. Lebezyatnikov reports that she cries, "People shall see the children of a noble family beg in the public streets!"

Sonya rushes out to find Katerina. Raskolnikov goes to his room, where Dunya soon comes to see him. She says that she has heard from Razumikhin of her brother's "persecution" by the police and pledges her support. Raskolnikov tells her that he thinks highly of Razumikhin. After she leaves, Raskolnikov goes out into the street, where Lebezyatnikov catches up with him and tells him that Katerina has truly gone mad and may soon be taken by the police. Lebezyatnikov leads Raskolnikov to Katerina and the children, around whom a crowd has formed. Katerina looks ghastly. She is obviously in the throes of her disease; she is animated by a mad energy, singing, dancing, and beating her children. She tries to appeal to the sympathies of well-dressed passersby, explaining that her children are of "noble, nay, even aristocratic family." She and the children are all crying. Katerina refuses Sonya's pleas that she return home. She has a confrontation with a policeman and coughs up a great deal of blood. She is taken back to their home, where she is laid on a couch. The policeman, Lebezyatnikov, Raskolnikov, Sonya, the children, the landlord, the landlady, and some strangers crowd around her as she dies. She refuses the services of a priest, saying she has no need for them. She starts having hallucinations. She calls for Sonya and, in a fit of convulsions, dies. Sonya, sobbing, throws herself onto the corpse.

Svidrigailov appears and tells Raskolnikov that he will use a portion of the money that he had promised Dunya to pay for a funeral and to provide for the children, who will be sent to an orphanage. He then reveals that he overheard Raskolnikov confessing the murders to Sonya.

ANALYSIS: CHAPTER V

This chapter centers on the climax of the Marmeladov subplot, with the frenzied death of Katerina Ivanovna. The combination of Luzhin's accusation of Sonya with the family's eviction by their landlady pushes Katerina over the edge, and she explodes in a frenzy of activity that culminates in her death. She desperately turns to illusions of her nobility and fantasies of the rich offering her support. When the rich treat her as badly as everyone else, however, it is more than her defenses can take, and she breaks down. In contrast to Raskolnikov, who accepts the deconstruction of the "superman" identity that he has envisioned for himself, Katerina defiantly plows through the reality that her proclaimed nobility is meaningless.

Although Katerina is delusional about the world around her, her sense of dignity is very real and quite strong. When her dignity bears the brunt of an intolerable attack, she responds by singing, dancing, and screaming her outrage against the world. Even her death, marked by sighs and convulsions, comes in a burst of activity. The juxtaposition of her grotesque behavior and repeated claims to nobility accentuates her obstinate refusal to alter her perception of herself in response to circumstances. Her pathetic claim to nobility becomes an increasingly angry assertion. On her deathbed, Katerina irritably refuses the services of a priest, declaring, "A priest? I am not in need of one. My conscience is free from sin! And, even were it not, God must forgive me. He knows how I have suffered!" Believing that her unending and highly visible tribulations have rendered her a martyr, Katerina believes that not even God can legitimately find fault with her.

This final portrait of Katerina Ivanovna completes the picture of the ruined Marmeladovs, a family that includes a drunk husband trampled to death in the streets, a proud but consumptive mother reduced to beating her children and begging, and an older daughter forced into prostitution. Sonya's suffering and devotion to her family stands out remarkably against this backdrop of utter despair. She has long understood and accepted her identity and role, despite the cruel and crushing reality of her life.

Svidrigailov's appearance at Katerina's deathbed moves the plot in two important directions. First, by offering to pay for the funeral and provide for Katerina's children, he frees Sonya from the overwhelming burden of caring for them, just as Razumikhin's willingness to care for Pulcheria Alexandrovna and Dunya enables Raskolnikov to separate himself from them without feeling that he is abandoning them. Second, Svidrigailov draws Raskolnikov into his web by revealing that he has overheard Raskolnikov's confession of the murders. He, Sonya, and Raskolnikov himself are now the only three people who know without a doubt that Raskolnikov is the murderer. While Sonya uses this knowledge for good—to try to persuade Raskolnikov to confess—it is unclear what Svidrigailov intends to do with it, but it is certain to be something much less honorable. Raskolnikov is losing control of his secret, and his control over events is about to unravel rapidly as well.

PART VI: CHAPTERS I–V

SUMMARY: CHAPTER I

A delirious haze settles over Raskolnikov in the days following Katerina Ivanovna's death and his confession to Sonya. He wanders the streets, hanging around in bars and outside the building in which Sonya lives. One day, Razumikhin comes to visit him in his room. He says that he has come to find out once and for all whether or not Raskolnikov has gone mad. Razumikhin decides that he has not. He tells Raskolnikov that Pulcheria Alexandrovna is heartbroken and feels abandoned. The always compassionate Razumikhin finally seems to have lost patience with Raskolnikov's selfishness, now that he has seen the pain that it causes his family. He informs Raskolnikov of a mysterious and upsetting letter that Dunya has received. He also mentions that Porfiry Petrovich apparently believes that the painter, Nikolai, is guilty of the murders. When Raskolnikov tells him of Dunya's earlier visit, Razumikhin becomes suspicious of a "conspiracy" between the two. After Razumikhin leaves, Porfiry appears.

SUMMARY: CHAPTER II

Porfiry tells Raskolnikov that he wants to apologize for his treatment of him, admitting that he was trying to extract a confession from him. He attributes his suspicions to Raskolnikov's article, his fainting on his first visit to the police station, and his remarks to Zamyotov at the Crystal Palace. But the official soon admits that he still does not believe Nikolai's confession, since the painter seems too childlike and is ignorant of most of the details of the crime.

Raskolnikov, Porfiry claims, is the true murderer. Raskolnikov denies the accusation, but Petrovich repeats the charge with confidence. He has not arrested Raskolnikov, he says, because he has not gathered enough evidence. He is sympathetic to Raskolnikov, he says, and urges him to confess. He claims that he has proof of Raskolnikov's guilt and that Raskolnikov would look better in the eyes of the judge if he confessed before the evidence was produced. If he confesses, Porfiry promises to put in a good word with the judge. He is confident that Raskolnikov's guilt will eventually cause him to confess. Before leaving, he asks Raskolnikov to leave a note disclosing the location of the stolen loot should he decide to commit suicide. Raskolnikov leaves his room soon after.

SUMMARY: CHAPTER III

Raskolnikov goes looking for Svidrigailov. He finds him in a café, being entertained in one of the back rooms by a singer. After a series of elusive exchanges with Svidrigailov, Raskolnikov, unsettled, threatens to kill him if he uses "some recent discovery" about Raskolnikov to force his will upon Dunya. Svidrigailov tells Raskolnikov that he enjoys observing him, and then begins to talk about his life. Thinking Svidrigailov a worthless and depraved man, Raskolnikov gets up to leave. Svidrigailov, however, persuades him to stay by mentioning Dunya.

SUMMARY: CHAPTER IV

Svidrigailov proceeds to tell Raskolnikov at length about his relationship with Marfa Petrovna, who allowed him to be unfaithful to her, and his attraction to Dunya. Raskolnikov notices that Svidrigailov is becoming drunk and announces that he is convinced that Svidrigailov still has designs on Dunya. Svidrigailov tries to deflect Raskolnikov's concerns by telling him that he has found himself a young, vulnerable fifteen-year-old girl and has recently become engaged to her. According to Svidrigailov, this girl possesses a mixture of childlike qualities and mature intelligence that he finds alluring. Raskolnikov is disgusted at the engagement and the depraved pleasure that the older man clearly takes in it, but Svidrigailov is unfazed. He leaves, amused by Raskolnikov's disapproval. Raskolnikov follows Svidrigailov into the street, worried that he might still be a threat to Dunya despite his engagement.

Summary: Chapter V

Svidrigailov notices Raskolnikov pursuing him and again tells him goodbye. Raskolnikov decides not to follow Svidrigailov after Svidrigailov boards a carriage for a distant part of the city. He fails to notice that Svidrigailov rides the carriage for only a hundred paces before getting off. Svidrigailov lures Dunya to his room by reminding her that he knows about her brother's secret, referring to the information that he promised to reveal in the mysterious letter mentioned by Razumikhin. Dunya is incredulous when Svidrigailov reveals that he overheard Raskolnikov confessing to the murders of Alyona Ivanovna and Lizaveta. While Dunya becomes faint with anger and confusion, Svidrigailov offers to help Raskolnikov avoid punishment if she will marry him. In horror, she runs to the door, only to discover that Svidrigailov has locked it. He threatens to rape her, warning that he can report her brother if she reports him. She pulls out a revolver, threatens him with it, and accuses him of poisoning his late wife. He dares her to fire, and she does, twice, but manages only to graze his temple. Svidrigailov moves to embrace her but, realizing that she will never love him, lets her go. Putting the revolver in his pocket, he goes out shortly thereafter.

Analysis: Chapters I–V

The mind game between Raskolnikov and Porfiry Petrovich reaches its climax in Part VI, Chapter II. Porfiry's shrewd expertise in psychology leads him to the bold move of declaring his suspicions to Raskolnikov. He guesses correctly that his suspect is tormented by his guilt. By placing the possibility of confession before Raskolnikov, he provides him with a method of resolving his unhappiness and thus appeals to his human side.

Svidrigailov embodies the qualities of immorality and self-absorption. Although he is human in a way that Luzhin and Raskolnikov are not, he greatly exceeds both in his capacity to be sneaky and calculating. While Luzhin is plainly nothing more than a cold, self-centered materialist, Svidrigailov is a complex character. His actions are ambiguous and his generosities can all be interpreted in ways that cast doubt on his good intentions. One can argue that his donation in support of the Marmeladov children is not, as it first seems, the kind gesture of a sinful but repentant man, but merely an attempt to get closer to Raskolnikov and, through him, Dunya. Conflicting stories about Svidrigailov's past, including whether he caused the death of one of his servants and whether he contributed to his wife's death, leave his motivations for his behavior in doubt.

Nonetheless, Svidrigailov's attempted rape of Dunya removes any lingering doubts about his character. But even here, the incident turns on more than just the pursuit of a goal. Although Dunya's gunshots cause no physical harm, they prove to Svidrigailov that she will never care for him. His subsequent urgency in asking her to leave evidences an intense inner struggle. He has managed to rein in, if only for a moment, the appetites that have driven him to sin in the past. Dostoevsky reveals that Svidrigailov, so often glib and cynical, suffers deeply when he sees his fantasy fractured. Svidrigailov's character adds depth and complexity to the novel's depiction of evil; in the extremity of his emotions, he is similar to the self-conscious, tormented Raskolnikov.

Dunya's use of the revolver in Chapter V presents a striking contrast to an earlier act of violence—the murders of Alyona and Lizaveta. Even with the justification of self-defense against an immediate physical threat, Dunya is unable to go through with the act, firing only twice before laying the gun down. Her unwillingness or inability to kill Svidrigailov renders irrelevant the philosophical rationalizations of murder that prompt Raskolnikov's actions. Dostoevsky seems to suggest that what matters is not whether the murder leads to the greatest good for the greatest number of people, but simply whether the individual with the gun can find it within him- or herself to kill another human being. Dunya clearly cannot, which distinguishes her from Raskolnikov.

Part VI: Chapters VI–VIII

Summary: Chapter VI

Svidrigailov wanders aimlessly around St. Petersburg, soaking himself in the rain. In the evening, he visits Sonya. He assures her that her siblings will be provided for and offers her a three-thousand-ruble bond. He tells her that she is to use the money to accompany Raskolnikov to Siberia. He himself is going off to America. After leaving Sonya, Svidrigailov visits his fiancée's family, informs them that he will be going away for some time, and presents them with fifteen thousand rubles. He then proceeds to a hotel, where he has feverish dreams, imagining that he has found a five-year-old girl in a corner of the hotel, whimpering from the cold. He lovingly puts her in her bed and wraps a blanket around her, but she turns to him with a depraved, seductive look on her face. He also dreams that rain is flooding St. Petersburg. He wakes just before dawn in a daze and goes out, taking Dunya's revolver with him. He finds a soldier keeping watch, puts the revolver to his head, and, before killing himself, tells the soldier to tell anyone who asks that he has gone to America.

SUMMARY: CHAPTER VII

Raskolnikov goes to see Pulcheria Alexandrovna. She says that she has read his article and was impressed by it, though she could not understand it all. Raskolnikov looks at the article with disgust. His mother has apparently convinced herself that her son is a genius destined for great things and that his eccentricities are all attributable to this fact. She is tearfully overjoyed to see him. Raskolnikov shocks her by asking if she will always love him no matter what. He tells her that he will always love her but that he must leave her. She tearfully tries to make him stay with her, but he leaves and returns to his apartment, where he finds Dunya waiting for him. He confesses to her that he contemplated suicide but could not go through with it. He tells her that he will confess, and she urges him to do so, arguing that it will help atone for his crime. But Raskolnikov becomes indignant. He argues that he only killed a "louse," and that if he had succeeded in profiting from his crime and doing some good by it, he would have nothing of which to be ashamed. Dunya is shocked at his response. Looking into her distraught face, he realizes how much pain he has brought to his family. The two go out, stopping to take one last look at each other as they walk in opposite directions.

SUMMARY: CHAPTER VIII

Raskolnikov goes to Sonya's lodging. The narrator tells us that Sonya and Dunya had become good friends during their visit the previous day, when Dunya discovered that Raskolnikov was guilty of the murders. Raskolnikov tells Sonya that he has come to pick up his cross. Sonya has him say a prayer before he leaves.

Raskolnikov starts walking toward the police station, dreading the public humiliation of a confession. He takes a detour to the Haymarket, remembering Sonya's suggestion that he declare his guilt at the crossroads. Along the way, he carefully observes every detail of the city around him, aware that he is taking his last look as a free man. At the Haymarket, he kisses the ground, but his action meets with jeers from the onlookers and he loses his nerve and decides not to confess publicly. But he then notices Sonya following him at a distance and feels renewed conviction. At the police station, he has a friendly chat with Ilya Petrovich, who apologizes for harboring suspicions about him. Ilya mentions Svidrigailov's suicide in passing, and Raskolnikov is so stunned that he leaves without confessing. But when he gets outside, he sees Sonya waiting for him, and he turns back into the police station and offers his confession to the shocked Ilya.

ANALYSIS: CHAPTERS VI–VIII

Svidrigailov's suicide sheds light on Raskolnikov's apparent inability to kill himself. Raskolnikov's disdain for humanity makes him think that suicide is a vulgar act reserved for common people (he earlier observes a suicide attempt with disgust). But though he is convinced, at times, that such an act is beneath him, it becomes clear that he lacks the moral strength to end his insidious life. Svidrigailov, on the other hand, is a realist; seeing his dreams fractured, he ends his life in a spree of utilitarian action—giving away money and removing a source of pain (himself) from Dunya's life. Raskolnikov hangs on to his idealism, unable to understand that killing himself would have been much more utilitarian than killing Alyona Ivanovna.

The climax of the Svidrigailov subplot occurs in Chapter VI, and the suspense surrounding Svidrigailov's true intentions builds in urgency until the last sentence of the chapter. Before he kills himself, Svidrigailov manages to tie up an important loose end in the plot, resolving the question of how Sonya can possibly act as Raskolnikov's companion when she has to support her younger siblings. Svidrigailov thus plays a critical practical role in the narrative. But even in the last minutes of his life, he is of great interest in his own right—a clearly cynical and depraved but also generous and enigmatic figure.

Raskolnikov's mother's desperate faith in her son's greatness adds poignancy to his decision to confess. Her pathetic attachment manifests itself in her being proud of her son's dreadful article ("On Crime"), a pride made all the more ridiculous by her admission that she didn't understand the article. The pain that she feels when he tells her that she cannot accompany him highlights their opposing views concerning the value of family relationships: while Pulcheria Alexandrovna, like Dunya and Sonya, places great weight on supportive relationships within the family, Raskolnikov shows concern for his family only in urgent circumstances, such as when he fears that Svidrigailov is planning to pursue Dunya aggressively. His ability to dismiss his mother somewhat callously, thinking first of his own needs, reveals the depth of his isolation from society.

Although Raskolnikov wonders why he visits Sonya before going to confess, it is clear to the reader that he needs to gather strength from her in order to go through with his confession. After he first leaves the police station, having failed to confess, it is the sight of Sonya, not the suspicions of the police or his own emotional turmoil, that pushes him to finally make his confession. Sonya is thus a pivotal character in the plot of the novel. Her crucial role in encouraging Raskolnikov to confess foreshadows her indispensability to Raskolnikov's eventual start toward redemption.

Raskolnikov's confession at the end of the main body of the novel constitutes the climax of *Crime and Punishment,* drawing the suspense surrounding the consequences of Raskolnikov's crime to a close. Even at the very end, Dostoevsky heightens the anticipation with the long, irrelevant conversation between Raskolnikov and Ilya Petrovich, and the outcome is temporarily cast into doubt when Raskolnikov turns and leaves the police station. The long-awaited confession does not come until nearly the last sentence of the last chapter. Subsequently, the uncertainty about Raskolnikov's fate drives the reader on to the Epilogue.

Epilogue

Summary: Chapter I

Raskolnikov is in prison in Siberia. He has been there for nine months, and a year and a half has passed since the murders. At his trial, Raskolnikov confessed to the crime, establishing his guilt by explaining why Lizaveta was murdered and identifying the location of the stolen goods. The examining magistrates and judges had trouble believing that Raskolnikov would not know how much money was in the stolen purse, which was hidden under the rock along with the pawned items, but the psychologists at the trial explained this ignorance as a symptom of his temporary insanity and "monomania." The testimony of his friends corroborated his deteriorated condition. Raskolnikov himself refused to offer or accept any defense of his actions, although he told the court that he sincerely repented his crime. He received a relatively light punishment, largely because Porfiry Petrovich kept silent about his knowledge of Raskolnikov's guilt, which enabled Raskolnikov to confess without being forced. He thereby saved Nikolai from wrongful punishment.

Razumikhin also testified to Raskolnikov's acts of charity while at the university, and his landlady testified about his heroism during a fire. Five months after first confessing, Raskolnikov was sentenced to eight years of hard labor in Siberia. Sonya went with him, while Razumikhin, Dunya, and Pulcheria Alexandrovna stayed in St. Petersburg. Before leaving St. Petersburg, Raskolnikov realized that his mother was on the verge of death.

Two months later, Razumikhin and Dunya married. They attempted to keep the truth about Raskolnikov's crime and imprisonment from his mother, but she eventually became delirious and died, revealing her knowledge of her son's fate before her death. Sonya serves as a link between the family in St. Petersburg and Raskolnikov in prison. She also lightens Raskolnikov's burden in the prison by winning favor with the authorities. Eventually, Raskolnikov falls dangerously ill and spends some time in the hospital.

Summary: Chapter II

> Infinite happiness lit up in her eyes . . . he loved her,
> loved her infinitely, and . . . at last the moment had
> come. . . .

(See QUOTATIONS, p. 67)

The narrator tells us that Raskolnikov does not mind the conditions of prison life but that his pride has been deeply wounded. He still believes that there was nothing wrong with his character and that what he did was not a sin but simply "an error." He considers his choice of confession over suicide the result of weakness rather than "a presentiment of future resurrection and a new life." The other prisoners don't like him much, though they adore Sonya. While Raskolnikov is ill, he has a dream that a virus is sweeping the country. The virus causes its victims to suffer a madness that causes each to think him- or herself the sole possessor of truth. People cannot get along and so tear each other apart.

Throughout Raskolnikov's imprisonment, Sonya comes to visit, sitting outside where Raskolnikov can see her from his window. One day, she manages to meet him outside. They sit next to each other for a moment, holding hands. Previously, when they had such opportunities and held hands, Raskolnikov felt a sense of revulsion. But this time is different. He collapses in tears and embraces her. They both realize that he truly loves her. They resolve to wait out the remaining seven years of his prison term. That evening, Raskolnikov thinks about Sonya and experiences the ecstasy of love. From underneath his pillow he takes a copy of the New Testament that Sonya had given him. He feels at one with her. The narrator closes the novel by stating that this man's renewal is the matter of another story.

ANALYSIS: CHAPTERS I–II

Some critics have argued that the Epilogue is an unnecessary and heavy-handed end to a novel that stands quite well without it. They criticize the dream of the virus spreading through Europe, the blossoming of Raskolnikov's love for Sonya, and the death of Raskolnikov's mother as blunt attempts to tie up the story and simplistic treatments of issues that the body of the novel deals with in much more complex and open-ended ways. This analysis notwithstanding, the Epilogue serves to develop several of the important themes of the novel, particularly those of alienation and religious redemption. At the end of Part VI, we are left in doubt as to the ultimate consequences of Raskolnikov's confession. The suspense that this doubt creates drives the reader into the Epilogue in search of answers. The descriptions of Raskolnikov's life in prison confirm that Raskolnikov, despite having confessed, is not yet truly repentant of his crime. Convinced that his crime was an "error," not a sin, he remains isolated from his fellow inmates, even as Sonya befriends them.

The recounting of the trial, a locus of objective analytical attitudes about Raskolnikov, demonstrates the disparity between Raskolnikov's perception of himself and others' perceptions of him. His friends testified to the degeneration of his mind, and the court officials assumed that he must be mentally deranged since he didn't even make use of the money and goods that he stole from Alyona. The testimonies of Razumikhin and the landlady about Raskolnikov's acts of goodness emphasize further how Raskolnikov's mental health was in serious decline by the time that he committed the murders. The narrator describes Raskolnikov's claims of repentance as exaggerated and coarse; Raskolnikov continues to cling to a belief in the morality, even nobility, of the murder of Alyona Ivanovna. Unwilling to let go of this belief, he is again forced to confront his mediocrity in the realm of the subconscious. His dream about the virus is aimed at stripping him of feelings of superiority, as the insanity and belief in the self as the sole possessor of truth infects everyone, thus dragging Raskolnikov back into the quagmire of banal humanity.

The scene in which Raskolnikov finally realizes that he loves Sonya, collapsing at her feet and weeping, is the first time that he is portrayed as being truly happy. Though the change in his character seems abrupt, it is the culmination of months of suffering and thought. Sonya's willingness to care for Raskolnikov, despite his frequent rudeness and apparent lack of love for her, demonstrates her enormously generous and self-sacrificing nature. Even as Raskolnikov keeps trying to reject human relationships, she serves as a link between him and Razumikhin and Dunya in St. Petersburg, and works to ease Raskolnikov's burden in the prison camp.

The theme of religious redemption is closely paired with that of reintegration into society. The cross that Sonya gives Raskolnikov in Part V, Chapter IV and the Bible that he begins to read in the Epilogue are both symbols of his awakening religious faith. Interestingly, faith is represented not as necessarily good in and of itself but rather as a way for Raskolnikov to reconnect with the people around him. Faith in God becomes a channel for him to bond with Sonya, just as the story of Lazarus resonates for both of them even when Raskolnikov explicitly rejects religious beliefs. Raskolnikov's reach for the New Testament as he revels in his newfound love suggests that this love will effect his Lazarus-like resurrection.

Important Quotations Explained

1. What was taking place in him was totally unfamiliar,
   new, sudden, never before experienced. Not that he
   understood it, but he sensed clearly, with all the power of
   sensation, that it was no longer possible for him to address
   these people in the police station, not only with heartfelt
   effusions, as he had just done, but in any way at all, and
   had they been his own brothers and sisters, and not police
   lieutenants, there would still have been no point in this
   addressing them, in whatever circumstances of life.

This quote, from Part II, Chapter I, illustrates Raskolnikov's sudden realization that by murdering Alyona and Lizaveta, he has completely isolated himself from society. His separation, which began before the murders, is now complete, as he has truly crossed over the bounds that formerly kept him tied to the rest of humanity. Indeed, one can argue that only because of his increasing alienation and lack of empathy for other people is Raskolnikov able to actually commit the murders. Additionally, the act of having physically accomplished the crime makes it necessary for Raskolnikov to cement his understanding of himself as a "superman" so that he can evade the bothersome, banal consequences of his actions. Much of the novel is concerned with Raskolnikov's gradual breakdown and deconstruction of this identity in the face of his alienation from others. Only when he confesses his guilt to Sonya, someone whom he sees as a fellow transgressor of morality, does he start on the path of rejoining society.

2. I've known Rodion for a year and a half: sullen, gloomy, arrogant, proud; recently (and maybe much earlier) insecure and hypochondriac. Magnanimous and kind. Doesn't like voicing his feelings, and would rather do something cruel than speak his heart out in words. At times, however, he's not hypochondriac at all, but just inhumanly cold and callous, as if there really were two opposite characters in him, changing places with each other. At times he's terribly taciturn! He's always in a hurry, always too busy, yet he lies there doing nothing. Not given to mockery, and not because he lacks sharpness but as if he had no time for such trifles. Never hears people out to the end. Is never interested in what interests everyone else at a given moment. Sets a terribly high value on himself and, it seems, not without a certain justification.

Razumikhin offers this description of Raskolnikov in Part III, Chapter II, to Sonya and Pulcheria Alexandrovna. His comments emphasize Raskolnikov's key character traits of self-centeredness, intelligence, and simultaneous cruelty and kindness. However, the informal, ungrammatical, and free-flowing tone of Razumikhin's remarks contributes to the seeming inconsistency of his words ("magnanimous and kind . . . inhumanly cold and callous"). The specific mention of "two opposite characters in him" seems to point to the unrelenting tension that Raskolnikov experiences as a result of his conflicting desire to confess and to evade capture. As a whole, this impressionistic depiction captures Raskolnikov's essential schismatic nature: he has detached himself from humanity and thus only engages in social behavior when it fits his needs.

Additionally, this passage sets up Razumikhin as Raskolnikov's foil, emphasizing the contrast between Razumikhin's friendliness and good nature and Raskolnikov's sullenness and antisocial nature. This difference constitutes strong counterevidence to the argument that Raskolnikov is compelled to commit the murders because of difficult circumstances in life. Razumikhin, like his friend, is a desperately poor ex-student, but he never even considers, much less commits, such a crime. To the contrary, he seems genuinely happy and takes a great deal of pleasure in life.

3.   The old woman was a mistake perhaps, but she's not the
     point! The old woman was merely a sickness . . . I was in
     a hurry to step over . . . it wasn't a human being I killed, it
     was a principle! So I killed the principle, but I didn't step
     over, I stayed on this side . . . All I managed to do was kill.
     And I didn't even manage that, as it turns out. . . .

This ranting comes from Part III, Chapter VI, when Raskolnikov
is lying in bed thinking to himself. The language, with its abrupt
phrases and frequent use of ellipses, reflects Raskolnikov's fractured
state of mind. It also shows that Raskolnikov is still trapped in a
Napoleonic mindset—he believes that the only thing that matters is
success in one's endeavors. Raskolnikov feels anxious not because
he is a murderer but because he is an unsuccessful murderer, unable to use the crime to his advantage and dismiss the guilt from his
mind. His need to assure himself of the intellectualized motivations
for Alyona Ivanovna's murder ("it wasn't a human being I killed,
it was a principle!") and his frantic, repetitive justification of his
crime ("I stayed on this side") reveal his insecurity about the whole
matter and accentuate how unlike his "superman" ideal he is. This
quote also foreshadows Raskolnikov's stubborn protest to Dunya
in Part VI, Chapter VII, that the murder itself was not wrong, only
his failure to profit from it.

QUOTATIONS

4.   What is it, to run away! A mere formality; that's not
        the main thing; no, he won't run away on me by a law
        of nature, even if he has somewhere to run to. Have
        you ever seen a moth near a candle? Well, so he'll keep
        circling around me, circling around me, as around a
        candle; freedom will no longer be dear to him, he'll fall to
        thinking, get entangled, he'll tangle himself all up as in a
        net, he'll worry himself to death! . . . he'll keep on making
        circles around me, narrowing the radius more and more,
        and—whop! He'll fly right into my mouth, and I'll swallow
        him, sir, and that will be most agreeable, heh, heh, heh!

Porfiry Petrovich speaks these words in Part IV, Chapter V, when
Raskolnikov goes to Porfiry's office with the ostensible purpose of
reclaiming his pawned possessions. This quotation gives the reader
a sense of Porfiry's style of speech, energetic to the point of being
frantic. It also demonstrates his method of focusing on the psychological aspects of the case, a method that seems to have been
Dostoevsky's as well. Porfiry's confidence that Raskolnikov "won't
run away on me by a law of nature"—that because he is human,
Raskolnikov ultimately will not be able to evade his guilt—provides
a sense of inevitability that Raskolnikov will either confess or go
mad. Additionally, in Dostoevsky's writing, every character serves
a specific function in the plot; we know that Porfiry's certainty of
Raskolnikov's guilt will not rest idle for long. This subtle tension
contributes to the novel's suspense throughout.

    Finally, Porfiry functions as a mirror for Raskolnikov. His dia-
tribe here seems tinged with the same obsessive, almost mad, tone as
Raskolnikov's monologues. He is the only character whose intelligence is a match for Raskolnikov's. As such, the magistrate seems at
times less like a real person and more like an imaginary conscience,
pointing out the moves of Raskolnikov's mind to Raskolnikov and
constantly reminding him that he will be found out eventually.

5.   How it happened he himself did not know, but suddenly
     it was as if something lifted him and flung him down at
     her feet. He wept and embraced her knees. For the first
     moment she was terribly frightened, and her whole face
     went numb. She jumped up and looked at him, trembling.
     But all at once, in that same moment, she understood
     everything. Infinite happiness lit up in her eyes; she
     understood, and for her there was no longer any doubt
     that he loved her, loved her infinitely, and that at last the
     moment had come. . . .

This quotation comes from the Epilogue, at the climactic moment
in which Sonya finally realizes that Raskolnikov truly loves her. The
significance is both personal and public, since by showing that he
loves a particular person, Raskolnikov demonstrates that he is willing to take his place as a member of society once again. The tears
that Raskolnikov sheds represent his remorse over his sins and, perhaps, his joy in realizing that Sonya, the lone individual with whom
he has enjoyed a meaningful relationship, loves him. It is only when
he realizes that he truly cares for another person that Raskolnikov
is finally able to break his alienation from humanity and begin to
sincerely repent for his crimes. This newfound love injects his life
with fresh meaning and, one can argue, releases him from the bond
of his destructive nihilism.

QUOTATIONS

KEY FACTS

FULL TITLE
Crime and Punishment

AUTHOR
Fyodor Dostoevsky

TYPE OF WORK
Novel

GENRE
Psychological drama

LANGUAGE
Russian

TIME AND PLACE WRITTEN
1865–1866, St. Petersburg, Russia

DATE OF FIRST PUBLICATION
1866; appeared serially in *The Russian Messenger* before being published in book form in 1867

PUBLISHER
The serial edition was published by the editor of *The Russian Messenger,* Mikhail Katkov; the two-volume book version was published by Bazanov.

NARRATOR
Third-person omniscient

CLIMAX
Raskolnikov's confession in Part VI, Chapter VIII

PROTAGONIST
Raskolnikov

ANTAGONISTS
Luzhin, Porfiry Petrovich, Svidrigailov, Raskolnikov's conscience

SETTINGS (TIME)
1860s

SETTINGS (PLACE)
St. Petersburg and a prison in Siberia

POINT OF VIEW
The story is told primarily from the point of view of
Raskolnikov but occasionally switches to the perspective of
Svidrigailov, Razumikhin, and Dunya.

FALLING ACTION
The Epilogue, in which Raskolnikov, imprisoned in Siberia,
discovers that he loves Sonya

TENSE
Past

FORESHADOWING
In Part I, Chapter I, when Raskolnikov rehearses the murder
of the pawnbroker; throughout the rest of the novel, whenever
Raskolnikov considers confessing

TONES
Tragic, emotional, melodramatic, critical, despairing, fatalistic,
confessional

THEMES
Alienation from society, the psychology of crime and
punishment, religious redemption, the importance of family,
nihilism, the "superman"

MOTIFS
Poverty

SYMBOLS
The city as a symbol of Raskolnikov's internal state; the cross as
a symbol of religious redemption

Study Questions

1. *Why does Raskolnikov kill the pawnbroker?*

Raskolnikov gives a number of different reasons for murdering Alyona, many of which involve pride. The clearest, most powerful reason seems to be a desire to prove his superiority to the rest of humanity. But he also claims, at times, that he committed the crime for utilitarian reasons—that the death of such a despicable "louse" would increase society's overall happiness—or that he did it solely out of a need for money. The narrator suggests in Part I that Raskolnikov's physical hunger, the squalid environment in which he lives, and his poor health may be responsible for weakening any impulses that might have prevented him from committing the murder.

Raskolnikov's deeper motivations for the murder are abstract, intellectual, and oddly rational. The discussion of Raskolnikov's article "On Crime" introduces the philosophical justifications for such a murder. In the article, Raskolnikov posits a class of "superm[e]n," who are superior, he argues, to the vast majority of humanity and thus have the right to violate moral codes. These ideas are strongly connected to nihilism, a philosophy rampant in late-nineteenth-century Russia that scorned traditional familial and societal bonds as well as emotional motivations. Central to nihilism was utilitarianism, the concept that moral decisions should be based on the rule of the greatest happiness for the largest number of people. Although the inner turmoil that Raskolnikov experiences from the moment that he commits the crime is a far cry from the superiority and righteousness with which the abstract "superman" is supposed to commit his crimes, Raskolnikov's justifications for the pawnbroker's murder are strongly utilitarian and nihilist.

2. *Discuss the development of the poverty motif over the course of the novel.*

Almost everyone in the novel is struggling for money and the pressing need of it serves as a constant reminder of unhappiness. Most striking are the poverty of Raskolnikov and that of Marmeladov and his family. Raskolnikov's poverty becomes part of his motivation for killing the pawnbroker, since he perceives of her death as a chance to get enough money to resume his education and make progress toward a better life. His poverty also, at least in his own mind, becomes a motivation for Dunya to marry Luzhin, though, of course, Dunya is motivated by her own poverty as well. The Marmeladovs' situation is obviously more severe. Marmeladov's drunkenness, Katerina Ivanovna's illness, and Sonya's turning to prostitution all vividly demonstrate the vicious cycle in which the economically and socially downtrodden are caught. Over the course of the novel, the causes and consequences of this kind of poverty are made increasingly clear, as various characters make sacrifices and important decisions based on their desperate need for money.

At the end of the novel, Svidrigailov's generosity changes the tone. Suddenly, and almost miraculously, everyone has enough money to do what he or she needs to do. One can interpret this sudden change either as an unrealistic deus ex machina—an obvious contrivance on the part of the author to salvage a seemingly hopeless situation for his or her characters—or as hopeful evidence of the power of faith, or at least good luck, to make the most important things in life possible.

3.   *Discuss Dostoevsky's use of coincidence as a plot*
       device in the novel. Does it affect the plausibility of the
       narrative? How does it affect the pacing?

Crime and Punishment abounds with coincidences. Two examples are Raskolnikov's overhearing of a discussion about killing
the pawnbroker, which solidifies his resolve to commit the murder, and his discovery of the injured Marmeladov in the street. The
first example is crucial to Raskolnikov's psychology. Although he is
extremely reluctant to kill Alyona before he overhears the conversation, one can argue that he truly desires to kill her and is simply
waiting for a sign that he is fated to do so. Support for this claim
can be found in the fact that when he overhears that Alyona will
be alone at home the next evening, he senses that circumstances
support his decision to commit the murder. Raskolnikov's pride is
tied up with what he interprets as coincidences and, even before the
murder, he is somewhat paranoid and ready to read deep meanings
into ostensibly trivial incidents.

   The coincidence of Raskolnikov coming across the just-injured
Marmeladov, on the other hand, makes no statement on his character. Rather, it serves primarily to advance the plot and give the
narrative an almost frantic feeling. In fact, seemingly at every turn,
Raskolnikov runs into some unexpected person or thing that drives
the plot onward. Nearly every event or encounter contributes to
the forward momentum of the plot, and the virtual lack of action-
less time periods in the novel gives it a rushed, delirious pacing that
serves to reflect Raskolnikov's own state of mind.

How to Write
Literary Analysis

The Literary Essay: A Step-by-Step Guide

When you read for pleasure, your only goal is enjoyment. You might find yourself reading to get caught up in an exciting story, to learn about an interesting time or place, or just to pass time. Maybe you're looking for inspiration, guidance, or a reflection of your own life. There are as many different, valid ways of reading a book as there are books in the world.

When you read a work of literature in an English class, however, you're being asked to read in a special way: you're being asked to perform *literary analysis*. To analyze something means to break it down into smaller parts and then examine how those parts work, both individually and together. Literary analysis involves examining all the parts of a novel, play, short story, or poem—elements such as character, setting, tone, and imagery—and thinking about how the author uses those elements to create certain effects.

A literary essay isn't a book review: you're not being asked whether or not you liked a book or whether you'd recommend it to another reader. A literary essay also isn't like the kind of book report you wrote when you were younger, where your teacher wanted you to summarize the book's action. A high school- or college-level literary essay asks, "How does this piece of literature actually work?" "How does it do what it does?" and, "Why might the author have made the choices he or she did?"

The Seven Steps
No one is born knowing how to analyze literature; it's a skill you learn and a process you can master. As you gain more practice with this kind of thinking and writing, you'll be able to craft a method that works best for you. But until then, here are seven basic steps to writing a well-constructed literary essay:

1. *Ask questions*
2. *Collect evidence*
3. *Construct a thesis*

4. Develop and organize arguments
5. Write the introduction
6. Write the body paragraphs
7. Write the conclusion

———————

1. Ask Questions

When you're assigned a literary essay in class, your teacher will often provide you with a list of writing prompts. Lucky you! Now all you have to do is choose one. Do yourself a favor and pick a topic that interests you. You'll have a much better (not to mention easier) time if you start off with something you enjoy thinking about. If you are asked to come up with a topic by yourself, though, you might start to feel a little panicked. Maybe you have too many ideas—or none at all. Don't worry. Take a deep breath and start by asking yourself these questions:

- **What struck you?** Did a particular image, line, or scene linger in your mind for a long time? If it fascinated you, chances are you can draw on it to write a fascinating essay.

- **What confused you?** Maybe you were surprised to see a character act in a certain way, or maybe you didn't understand why the book ended the way it did. Confusing moments in a work of literature are like a loose thread in a sweater: if you pull on it, you can unravel the entire thing. Ask yourself why the author chose to write about that character or scene the way he or she did and you might tap into some important insights about the work as a whole.

- **Did you notice any patterns?** Is there a phrase that the main character uses constantly or an image that repeats throughout the book? If you can figure out how that pattern weaves through the work and what the significance of that pattern is, you've almost got your entire essay mapped out.

- **Did you notice any contradictions or ironies?** Great works of literature are complex; great literary essays recognize and explain those complexities. Maybe the title (*Happy Days*) totally disagrees with the book's subject matter (hungry orphans dying in the woods). Maybe the main character acts one way around his family and a completely different way around his friends and associates. If you can find a way to explain a work's contradictory elements, you've got the seeds of a great essay.

At this point, you don't need to know exactly what you're going to say about your topic; you just need a place to begin your exploration. You can help direct your reading and brainstorming by formulating your topic as a *question,* which you'll then try to answer in your essay. The best questions invite critical debates and discussions, not just a rehashing of the summary. Remember, you're looking for something you can *prove or argue* based on evidence you find in the text. Finally, remember to keep the scope of your question in mind: is this a topic you can adequately address within the word or page limit you've been given? Conversely, is this a topic big enough to fill the required length?

GOOD QUESTIONS

"Are Romeo and Juliet's parents responsible for the deaths of their children?"
"Why do pigs keep showing up in LORD OF THE FLIES*?"*
"Are Dr. Frankenstein and his monster alike? How?"

BAD QUESTIONS

"What happens to Scout in TO KILL A MOCKINGBIRD*?"*
"What do the other characters in JULIUS CAESAR *think about Caesar?"*
"How does Hester Prynne in THE SCARLET LETTER *remind me of my sister?"*

---

2. COLLECT EVIDENCE

Once you know what question you want to answer, it's time to scour the book for things that will help you answer the question. Don't worry if you don't know what you want to say yet—right now you're just collecting ideas and material and letting it all percolate. Keep track of passages, symbols, images, or scenes that deal with your topic. Eventually, you'll start making connections between these examples and your thesis will emerge.

Here's a brief summary of the various parts that compose each and every work of literature. These are the elements that you will analyze in your essay, and which you will offer as evidence to support your arguments. For more on the parts of literary works, see the Glossary of Literary Terms at the end of this section.

ELEMENTS OF STORY   These are the *what*s of the work—what happens, where it happens, and to whom it happens.

- **Plot:** All of the events and actions of the work.

- **Character:** The people who act and are acted upon in a literary work. The main character of a work is known as the *protagonist.*

- **Conflict:** The central tension in the work. In most cases, the protagonist wants something, while opposing forces (antagonists) hinder the protagonist's progress.

- **Setting:** When and where the work takes place. Elements of setting include location, time period, time of day, weather, social atmosphere, and economic conditions.

- **Narrator:** The person telling the story. The narrator may straightforwardly report what happens, convey the subjective opinions and perceptions of one or more characters, or provide commentary and opinion in his or her own voice.

- **Themes:** The main idea or message of the work—usually an abstract idea about people, society, or life in general. A work may have many themes, which may be in tension with one another.

ELEMENTS OF STYLE   These are the *how*s—how the characters speak, how the story is constructed, and how language is used throughout the work.

- **Structure and organization:** How the parts of the work are assembled. Some novels are narrated in a linear, chronological fashion, while others skip around in time. Some plays follow a traditional three- or five-act structure, while others are a series of loosely connected scenes. Some authors deliberately leave gaps in their works, leaving readers to puzzle out the missing information. A work's structure and organization can tell you a lot about the kind of message it wants to convey.

- **Point of view:** The perspective from which a story is told. In *first-person point of view,* the narrator involves him or herself in the story. ("I went to the store"; "We watched in horror as the bird slammed into the window.") A first-person narrator is usually the protagonist of the work, but not always. In *third-person point of view,* the narrator does not participate in the story. A third-person narrator may closely follow a specific character, recounting that individual character's thoughts or experiences, or it may be what we call an *omniscient* narrator. Omniscient narrators see and know all: they can witness any event in any time or place and are privy to the inner thoughts and feelings of all characters. Remember that the narrator and the author are not the same thing!

- **Diction:** Word choice. Whether a character uses dry, clinical language or flowery prose with lots of exclamation points can tell you a lot about his or her attitude and personality.

- **Syntax:** Word order and sentence construction. Syntax is a crucial part of establishing an author's narrative voice. Ernest Hemingway, for example, is known for writing in very short, straightforward sentences, while James Joyce characteristically wrote in long, incredibly complicated lines.

- **Tone:** The mood or feeling of the text. Diction and syntax often contribute to the tone of a work. A novel written in short, clipped sentences that use small, simple words might feel brusque, cold, or matter-of-fact.

- **Imagery:** Language that appeals to the senses, representing things that can be seen, smelled, heard, tasted, or touched.

- **Figurative language:** Language that is not meant to be interpreted literally. The most common types of figurative language are *metaphors* and *similes,* which compare two unlike things in order to suggest a similarity between them— for example, "All the world's a stage," or "The moon is like a ball of green cheese." (Metaphors say one thing *is* another thing; similes claim that one thing is *like* another thing.)

---

3. CONSTRUCT A THESIS

When you've examined all the evidence you've collected and know how you want to answer the question, it's time to write your thesis statement. A *thesis* is a claim about a work of literature that needs to be supported by evidence and arguments. The thesis statement is the heart of the literary essay, and the bulk of your paper will be spent trying to prove this claim. A good thesis will be:

- **Arguable.** "*The Great Gatsby* describes New York society in the 1920s" isn't a thesis—it's a fact.

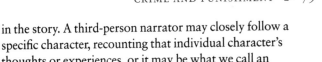

LITERARY ANALYSIS

- **Provable through textual evidence**. "*Hamlet* is a confusing but ultimately very well-written play" is a weak thesis because it offers the writer's personal opinion about the book. Yes, it's arguable, but it's not a claim that can be proved or supported with examples taken from the play itself.

- **Surprising**. "Both George and Lenny change a great deal in *Of Mice and Men*" is a weak thesis because it's obvious. A really strong thesis will argue for a reading of the text that is not immediately apparent.

- **Specific**. "Dr. Frankenstein's monster tells us a lot about the human condition" is *almost* a really great thesis statement, but it's still too vague. What does the writer mean by "a lot"? *How* does the monster tell us so much about the human condition?

GOOD THESIS STATEMENTS

Question: In *Romeo and Juliet*, which is more powerful in shaping the lovers' story: fate or foolishness?

Thesis: "Though Shakespeare defines Romeo and Juliet as 'star-crossed lovers' and images of stars and planets appear throughout the play, a closer examination of that celestial imagery reveals that the stars are merely witnesses to the characters' foolish activities and not the causes themselves."

Question: How does the bell jar function as a symbol in Sylvia Plath's *The Bell Jar*?

Thesis: "A bell jar is a bell-shaped glass that has three basic uses: to hold a specimen for observation, to contain gases, and to maintain a vacuum. The bell jar appears in each of these capacities in *The Bell Jar*, Plath's semi-autobiographical novel, and each appearances marks a different stage in Esther's mental breakdown."

Question: Would Piggy in *The Lord of the Flies* make a good island leader if he were given the chance?

Thesis: "Though the intelligent, rational, and innovative Piggy has the mental characteristics of a good leader, he ultimately lacks the social skills necessary to be an effective one. Golding emphasizes this point by giving Piggy a foil in the charismatic Jack, whose magnetic personality allows him to capture and wield power effectively, if not always wisely."

4. Develop and Organize Arguments

The reasons and examples that support your thesis will form the middle paragraphs of your essay. Since you can't really write your thesis statement until you know how you'll structure your argument, you'll probably end up working on steps 3 and 4 at the same time.

There's no single method of argumentation that will work in every context. One essay prompt might ask you to compare and contrast two characters, while another asks you to trace an image through a given work of literature. These questions require different kinds of answers and therefore different kinds of arguments. Below, we'll discuss three common kinds of essay prompts and some strategies for constructing a solid, well-argued case.

Types of Literary Essays

- **Compare and contrast**

    Compare and contrast the characters of Huck and Jim in The Adventures of Huckleberry Finn.

    Chances are you've written this kind of essay before. In an academic literary context, you'll organize your arguments the same way you would in any other class. You can either go *subject by subject* or *point by point*. In the former, you'll discuss one character first and then the second. In the latter, you'll choose several traits (attitude toward life, social status, images and metaphors associated with the character) and devote a paragraph to each. You may want to use a mix of these two approaches—for example, you may want to spend a paragraph a piece broadly sketching Huck's and Jim's personalities before transitioning into a paragraph or two that describes a few key points of comparison. This can be a highly effective strategy if you want to make a counterintuitive argument—that, despite seeming to be totally different, the two objects being compared are actually similar in a very important way (or vice versa). Remember that your essay should reveal something fresh or unexpected about the text, so think beyond the obvious parallels and differences.

- **Trace**

    Choose an image—for example, birds, knives, or eyes—and trace that image throughout Macbeth.

    Sounds pretty easy, right? All you need to do is read the play, underline every appearance of a knife in *Macbeth,* and then list them in your essay in the order they appear, right? Well, not exactly. Your teacher doesn't want a simple catalog of examples. He or she wants to see you make *connections* between those examples—that's the difference between summarizing and analyzing. In the *Macbeth* example above, think about the different contexts in which knives appear in the play and to what effect. In *Macbeth,* there are real knives and imagined knives; knives that kill and knives that simply threaten. Categorize and classify your examples to give them some order. Finally, always keep the overall effect in mind. After you choose and analyze your examples, you should come to some greater understanding about the work, as well as your chosen image, symbol, or phrase's role in developing the major themes and stylistic strategies of that work.

- **Debate**

    Is the society depicted in 1984 *good for its citizens?*

    In this kind of essay, you're being asked to debate a moral, ethical, or aesthetic issue regarding the work. You might be asked to judge a character or group of characters (*Is Caesar responsible for his own demise?*) or the work itself (*Is* JANE EYRE *a feminist novel?*). For this kind of essay, there are two important points to keep in mind. First, don't simply base your arguments on your personal feelings and reactions. Every literary essay expects you to read and analyze the work, so search for evidence in the text. What do characters in *1984* have to say about the government of Oceania? What images does Orwell use that might give you a hint about his attitude toward the government? As in any debate, you also need to make sure that you define all the necessary terms before you begin to argue your case. What does it mean to be a "good" society? What makes a novel "feminist"? You should define your terms right up front, in the first paragraph after your introduction.

    Second, remember that strong literary essays make contrary and surprising arguments. Try to think outside the box. In the *1984* example above, it seems like the obvious answer would be no, the totalitarian society depicted in Orwell's novel is *not* good for its citizens. But can you think of any arguments for the opposite side? Even if your final assertion is that the novel depicts a cruel, repressive, and therefore harmful society, acknowledging and responding to the counterargument will strengthen your overall case.

5. WRITE THE INTRODUCTION

Your introduction sets up the entire essay. It's where you present your topic and articulate the particular issues and questions you'll be addressing. It's also where you, as the writer, introduce yourself to your readers. A persuasive literary essay immediately establishes its writer as a knowledgeable, authoritative figure.

An introduction can vary in length depending on the overall length of the essay, but in a traditional five-paragraph essay it should be no longer than one paragraph. However long it is, your introduction needs to:

- **Provide any necessary context.** Your introduction should situate the reader and let him or her know what to expect. What book are you discussing? Which characters? What topic will you be addressing?

- **Answer the "So what?" question.** Why is this topic important, and why is your particular position on the topic noteworthy? Ideally, your introduction should pique the reader's interest by suggesting how your argument is surprising or otherwise counterintuitive. Literary essays make unexpected connections and reveal less-than-obvious truths.

- **Present your thesis.** This usually happens at or very near the end of your introduction.

- **Indicate the shape of the essay to come.** Your reader should finish reading your introduction with a good sense of the scope of your essay as well as the path you'll take toward proving your thesis. You don't need to spell out every step, but you do need to suggest the organizational pattern you'll be using.

Your introduction should not:

- **Be vague.** Beware of the two killer words in literary analysis: *interesting* and *important*. Of course the work, question, or example is interesting and important—that's why you're writing about it!

- **Open with any grandiose assertions.** Many student readers think that beginning their essays with a flamboyant statement such as, "Since the dawn of time, writers have been fascinated with the topic of free will," makes them sound important and commanding. You know what? It actually sounds pretty amateurish.

- **Wildly praise the work.** Another typical mistake student writers make is extolling the work or author. Your teacher doesn't need to be told that "Shakespeare is perhaps the greatest writer in the English language." You can mention a work's reputation in passing—by referring to *The Adventures of Huckleberry Finn* as "Mark Twain's enduring classic," for example—but don't make a point of bringing it up unless that reputation is key to your argument.

- **Go off-topic.** Keep your introduction streamlined and to the point. Don't feel the need to throw in all kinds of bells and whistles in order to impress your reader—just get to the point as quickly as you can, without skimping on any of the required steps.

---

6. WRITE THE BODY PARAGRAPHS

Once you've written your introduction, you'll take the arguments you developed in step 4 and turn them into your body paragraphs. The organization of this middle section of your essay will largely be determined by the argumentative strategy you use, but no matter how you arrange your thoughts, your body paragraphs need to do the following:

- **Begin with a strong topic sentence.** Topic sentences are like signs on a highway: they tell the reader where they are and where they're going. A good topic sentence not only alerts readers to what issue will be discussed in the following paragraph but also gives them a sense of what argument will be made *about* that issue. "Rumor and gossip play an important role in *The Crucible*" isn't a strong topic sentence because it doesn't tell us very much. "The community's constant gossiping creates an environment that allows false accusations to flourish" is a much stronger topic sentence— it not only tells us *what* the paragraph will discuss (gossip) but *how* the paragraph will discuss the topic (by showing how gossip creates a set of conditions that leads to the play's climactic action).

- **Fully and completely develop a single thought.** Don't skip around in your paragraph or try to stuff in too much material. Body paragraphs are like bricks: each individual

one needs to be strong and sturdy or the entire structure
will collapse. Make sure you have really proven your point
before moving on to the next one.

- **Use transitions effectively.** Good literary essay writers know
that each paragraph must be clearly and strongly linked to
the material around it. Think of each paragraph as a response
to the one that precedes it. Use transition words and phrases
such as *however, similarly, on the contrary, therefore,* and
furthermore to indicate what kind of response you're making.

---

7. WRITE THE CONCLUSION

Just as you used the introduction to ground your readers in the topic
before providing your thesis, you'll use the conclusion to quickly
summarize the specifics learned thus far and then hint at the broader
implications of your topic. A good conclusion will:

- **Do more than simply restate the thesis.** If your thesis argued
that *The Catcher in the Rye* can be read as a Christian
allegory, don't simply end your essay by saying, "And that
is why *The Catcher in the Rye* can be read as a Christian
allegory." If you've constructed your arguments well, this
kind of statement will just be redundant.

- **Synthesize the arguments, not summarize them.** Similarly,
don't repeat the details of your body paragraphs in your
conclusion. The reader has already read your essay, and
chances are it's not so long that they've forgotten all your
points by now.

- **Revisit the "So what?" question.** In your introduction,
you made a case for why your topic and position are
important. You should close your essay with the same sort
of gesture. What do your readers know now that they didn't
know before? How will that knowledge help them better
appreciate or understand the work overall?

- **Move from the specific to the general.** Your essay has most
likely treated a very specific element of the work—a single
character, a small set of images, or a particular passage. In
your conclusion, try to show how this narrow discussion has
wider implications for the work overall. If your essay on *To
Kill a Mockingbird* focused on the character of Boo Radley,
for example, you might want to include a bit in your

conclusion about how he fits into the novel's larger message about childhood, innocence, or family life.

- **Stay relevant.** Your conclusion should suggest new directions of thought, but it shouldn't be treated as an opportunity to pad your essay with all the extra, interesting ideas you came up with during your brainstorming sessions but couldn't fit into the essay proper. Don't attempt to stuff in unrelated queries or too many abstract thoughts.

- **Avoid making overblown closing statements.** A conclusion should open up your highly specific, focused discussion, but it should do so without drawing a sweeping lesson about life or human nature. Making such observations may be part of the point of reading, but it's almost always a mistake in essays, where these observations tend to sound overly dramatic or simply silly.

A+ Essay Checklist

Congratulations! If you've followed all the steps we've outlined above, you should have a solid literary essay to show for all your efforts. What if you've got your sights set on an A+? To write the kind of superlative essay that will be rewarded with a perfect grade, keep the following rubric in mind. These are the qualities that teachers expect to see in a truly A+ essay. How does yours stack up?

✓ Demonstrates a thorough understanding of the book

✓ Presents an original, compelling argument

✓ Thoughtfully analyzes the text's formal elements

✓ Uses appropriate and insightful examples

✓ Structures ideas in a logical and progressive order

✓ Demonstrates a mastery of sentence construction, transitions, grammar, spelling, and word choice

Suggested Essay Topics

1. Describe the importance of the city to the plot. How does the city serve as a symbol of society and of Raskolnikov's state of mind?

2. What impact do the descriptions of the various apartments— including those of Raskolnikov, Alyona, Sonya, Luzhin, and Dunya and Pulcheria Alexandrovna—have on our understanding of the characters who inhabit them and the events that take place within them?

3. Compare the characters of Raskolnikov and Razumikhin. How does Razumikhin describe Raskolnikov, and vice versa? Does Razumikhin serve as Raskolnikov's foil? Are there other characters who are foils to Raskolnikov?

4. Discuss the use of foreshadowing in the novel. How does foreshadowing increase the level of suspense? Are there times when knowing what will happen later decreases the suspense? What effect does having the murder occur at the very beginning have on the structure of the novel?

5. Lebezyatnikov spouts a variety of theories about society. What role does he play in the novel? How might his character reflect Dostoevsky's own political experiences?

6. Discuss the development of the theme of religious redemption over the course of the novel.

A+ Student Essay

> If a hero is defined as a man or woman with noble
> attributes who carries out difficult and frightening tasks, to
> what extent is Raskolnikov a hero?

At first glance, Raskolnikov seems the opposite of a hero. He murders a defenseless old woman, then insists he has done nothing wrong. Still, his conscience torments him: He worries about his actions, his family, and the nation in which he lives. Because he thinks deeply about moral problems, Raskolnikov is ultimately able to commit brave acts, turning himself into the police and atoning for his sinful past. Though Raskolnikov spends most of the novel in a decidedly non-heroic state, his keen, searching conscience allows him to attain grace in the closing epilogue and he ends the novel a hero.

To be sure, Raskolnikov engages in numerous unheroic thoughts and deeds. Toward the beginning of the novel, he attacks and kills the moneylender Alyona Ivanovna. He tells himself he has behaved admirably; by his perverse logic, moneylenders are so cruel that they do not deserve to live. "Crime?" he says. "What crime?" He likens Alyona Ivanova to a "louse" that has "sucked the life-sap from the poor," and claims that killing her was a virtuous act that should earn him forgiveness for forty sins. Raskolnikov also develops a worldview in which some men are so farsighted and brilliant that they may kill anyone who displeases them, counting himself as one of these men. This pattern of selfish thoughts and actions certainly does not seem heroic.

On the other hand, Raskolnikov's active conscience distinguishes him from most people. The guilt he feels after killing Alyona Ivanovna is the most brutal punishment in the novel. Even the police investigator, Porfiry Petrovich, admires Raskolnikov for his finely-tuned sensibilities. His conscience causes him to worry not just about his own sins, but also about the sins of nineteenth-century Russia. He refuses to marry, seeing the institution as deeply flawed and imbalanced, and he forbids his sister to marry Luzhin because such a marriage would reduce her to a servant. The status of Russian women enrages him and his heart aches for Sonya, who prostitutes herself to feed her family. Tormented, he dreams of a poor, weak horse that gets crushed in the street. To Raskolnikov, the horse represents Russia's starving masses, sacrificed in the name of progress.

These moments of bitterness and idealism show that Raskolnikov has an extraordinary conscience.

Raskolnikov's active, well-developed conscience ultimately enables him to commit heroic acts. These acts of heroism occur toward the very end of the novel, after the psychological torment proves too much to bear and he turns himself in. Sentenced to hard labor in Siberia, the young man accepts his fate with surprising courage and grace. Though it doesn't happen immediately, Raskolnikov eventually renounces his selfish thoughts and realizes that he had allowed himself to become alienated from the human community. The resolute loner even declares his love for the steadfast Sonya, an act of pure faith from a man who has despised marriage for so long. "Instead of dialectics," Dostoyevsky writes, Raskolnikov realizes that "there was life, and something different to work itself out in his consciousness." He changes from a self-pitying criminal into a generous, compassionate man, capable of loving another person.

It may seem strange to call a murderer heroic. But Dostoyevsky persuades us that Raskolnikov has undergone a beautiful transformation—from peevish liar to mature and penitent man. Raskolnikov has the courage to examine his past, admit that some of his beliefs are wrongheaded, and change the way he thinks and acts, and in so doing he undertakes a daunting, rare, and admirable journey—a journey that can certainly be described as an act of heroism.

GLOSSARY OF LITERARY TERMS

ANTAGONIST

The entity that acts to frustrate the goals of the *protagonist*. The antagonist is usually another *character* but may also be a non-human force.

ANTIHERO / ANTIHEROINE

A *protagonist* who is not admirable or who challenges notions of what should be considered admirable.

CHARACTER

A person, animal, or any other thing with a personality that appears in a *narrative*.

CLIMAX

The moment of greatest intensity in a text or the major turning point in the *plot*.

CONFLICT

The central struggle that moves the *plot* forward. The conflict can be the *protagonist*'s struggle against fate, nature, society, or another person.

FIRST-PERSON POINT OF VIEW

A literary style in which the *narrator* tells the story from his or her own *point of view* and refers to himself or herself as "I." The narrator may be an active participant in the story or just an observer.

HERO / HEROINE

The principal *character* in a literary work or *narrative*.

IMAGERY

Language that brings to mind sense-impressions, representing things that can be seen, smelled, heard, tasted, or touched.

MOTIF

A recurring idea, structure, contrast, or device that develops or informs the major *themes* of a work of literature.

NARRATIVE

A story.

NARRATOR

The person (sometimes a *character*) who tells a story; the *voice* assumed by the writer. The narrator and the author of the work of literature are not the same person.

PLOT

The arrangement of the events in a story, including the sequence in which they are told, the relative emphasis they are given, and the causal connections between events.

POINT OF VIEW

The *perspective* that a *narrative* takes toward the events it describes.

PROTAGONIST

The main *character* around whom the story revolves.

SETTING

The location of a *narrative* in time and space. Setting creates mood or atmosphere.

SUBPLOT

A secondary *plot* that is of less importance to the overall story but may serve as a point of contrast or comparison to the main plot.

SYMBOL

An object, *character,* figure, or color that is used to represent an abstract idea or concept. Unlike an *emblem,* a symbol may have different meanings in different contexts.

SYNTAX

The way the words in a piece of writing are put together to form lines, phrases, or clauses; the basic structure of a piece of writing.

THEME

A fundamental and universal idea explored in a literary work.

TONE

The author's attitude toward the subject or *characters* of a story or poem or toward the reader.

VOICE

An author's individual way of using language to reflect his or her own personality and attitudes. An author communicates voice through *tone, diction,* and *syntax.*

LITERARY ANALYSIS

A NOTE ON PLAGIARISM

Plagiarism—presenting someone else's work as your own—rears its ugly head in many forms. Many students know that copying text without citing it is unacceptable. But some don't realize that even if you're not quoting directly, but instead are paraphrasing or summarizing, *it is plagiarism* unless you cite the source.

Here are the most common forms of plagiarism:

- Using an author's phrases, sentences, or paragraphs without citing the source
- Paraphrasing an author's ideas without citing the source
- Passing off another student's work as your own

How do you steer clear of plagiarism? You should *always* acknowledge all words and ideas that aren't your own by using quotation marks around verbatim text or citations like footnotes and endnotes to note another writer's ideas. For more information on how to give credit when credit is due, ask your teacher for guidance or visit www.sparknotes.com.

LITERARY ANALYSIS

REVIEW & RESOURCES

QUIZ

1. From whom does Raskolnikov get the ax that he uses to kill
    Alyona Ivanovna and Lizaveta?

    A. A stranger
    B. The caretaker
    C. Nastasya
    D. Razumikhin

2. Why is Raskolnikov immediately opposed to the marriage of
    his sister to Luzhin?

    A. He doesn't believe that Luzhin earns enough to
        support a family.
    B. He wants her to marry Razumikhin instead.
    C. He thinks that she is sacrificing herself for the sake of
        Luzhin's money.
    D. He is against marriage in general.

3. When Raskolnikov first meets him, why is Marmeladov
    afraid to return to his home?

    A. He has been on a five-day drinking binge and cannot
        face his family.
    B. He is afraid of contracting tuberculosis from his wife,
        Katerina Ivanovna.
    C. He is worried that the authorities will arrest him.
    D. None of the above

4. Why does Raskolnikov kill Lizaveta?

    A. He dislikes her.
    B. She is trying to prevent him from stealing the
        pawnbroker's money.
    C. She attacks him in an attempt to revenge her sister.
    D. She is a witness to the murder of her sister.

5. What does Sonya do to support her family?

   A. Sews
   B. Steals
   C. Begs
   D. Prostitutes herself

6. What is Porfiry Petrovich's first clue that Raskolnikov might be the killer?

   A. Raskolnikov faints at the police station during a conversation about the murder.
   B. Raskolnikov returns to the pawnbroker's apartment and asks about blood.
   C. Raskolnikov becomes delirious the day after the murder.
   D. Raskolnikov teases Zamyotov about the possibility that he is the murderer.

7. *Crime and Punishment* was initially published in

   A. 1862
   B. 1864
   C. 1866
   D. 1868

8. Where does Raskolnikov meet the drunk civil official Marmeladov?

   A. In Raskolnikov's apartment
   B. In Marmeladov's apartment
   C. In the street
   D. In a tavern

9. What event tarnished Dunya's reputation in her hometown?

   A. Rumors that she had become a prostitute to support herself and her mother
   B. Rumors that she made improper advances toward Svidrigailov
   C. The breaking of her engagement with Luzhin
   D. Rumors that her brother had committed a murder

10. What does Raskolnikov overhear in the Haymarket that clinches his resolve to kill Alyona?

    A.   A conversation about how the death of the pawnbroker would be a boon to society

    B.   A conversation indicating that Alyona will be alone in her apartment the next evening

    C.   The mention of an ax in the caretaker's shed

    D.   That Alyona is one of the wealthiest women in Russia

11. Where does Raskolnikov ultimately hide the goods that he steals from Alyona?

    A.   Under the couch in his apartment

    B.   In Sonya's apartment

    C.   Under a rock in a vacant courtyard

    D.   At the bottom of the Neva River

12. Which nightmare does Raskolnikov mistake for reality, even after waking up?

    A.   The dream in which he tries to murder Alyona

    B.   The dream in which Ilya Petrovich is beating Raskolnikov's landlady

    C.   The dream in which a small boy tries to keep a horse from being beaten

    D.   The dream in which a plague of selfishness and pride spreads across Europe

13. Who takes care of Raskolnikov during his sickness after the murder?

    A.   Razumikhin and Nastasya

    B.   Dunya and Nastasya

    C.   Razumikhin, Dunya, and Nastasya

    D.   Pulcheria Alexandrovna, Dunya, and Razumikhin

14. What is the name of the café in which Raskolnikov jokes with Zamyotov about having murdered Alyona and Lizaveta?

    A. The Boar's Head
    B. Bakaleev's
    C. The Neva
    D. The Crystal Palace

15. How does Marmeladov die?

    A. He shoots himself.
    B. He is trampled under a horse-drawn carriage.
    C. He dies of consumption.
    D. He dies of alcohol poisoning.

16. What is the main reason that Sonya first visits Raskolnikov in his apartment?

    A. She is attracted to him.
    B. She wants to thank him for the money that he gave to Katerina Ivanovna.
    C. She wants to invite him to the memorial dinner for her father.
    D. Raskolnikov wants to talk to her about the murders.

17. During their first conversation, what question does Porfiry Petrovich ask Raskolnikov that he thinks is a trap?

    A. Whether he had ever been to Alyona's apartment
    B. Whether he knew the pawnbroker's sister Lizaveta
    C. Whether there were painters in the apartment building when he pawned his watch
    D. Whether he thought that extraordinary people had the right to transgress accepted standards of morality

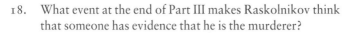

18. What event at the end of Part III makes Raskolnikov think that someone has evidence that he is the murderer?

    A.   A stranger comes up to him outside of his apartment and calls him a murderer.

    B.   Porfiry Petrovich asks him a series of leading questions.

    C.   Razumikhin tells him that the police suspect him.

    D.   Raskolnikov discovers that the police had searched his apartment while he was talking to Porfiry Petrovich.

19. What does Svidrigailov say during their first conversation that convinces Raskolnikov that Svidrigailov is losing his mind?

    A.   He tells Raskolnikov that he is in love with Dunya.

    B.   He tells Raskolnikov of his dream about a depraved five-year-old girl.

    C.   He tells Raskolnikov that the ghost of his dead wife, Marfa, appears to him.

    D.   He tells Raskolnikov that he knows he is the murderer.

20. Why does Dunya break her engagement with Luzhin?

    A.   Because he insults Razumikhin

    B.   Because he implies that Dunya is having a relationship with Svidrigailov

    C.   Because he insults Pulcheria Alexandrovna

    D.   Because he is stingy, overbearing, and dislikes Raskolnikov

21. What business does Razumikhin propose that he, Dunya, and Raskolnikov go into?

    A.   Law

    B.   Running an orphanage

    C.   Publishing

    D.   Running a restaurant

22. What biblical story does Raskolnikov order Sonya to read to him?

    A. The story of Genesis
    B. The story of the Sermon on the Mount
    C. The story of the Crucifixion
    D. The story of Lazarus

23. What is the name of the painter who confesses to the murders just as Raskolnikov is about to break under Porfiry Petrovich's pressure?

    A. Nikolai
    B. Misha
    C. Alyosha
    D. Ivan

24. How does Luzhin try to discredit Sonya and, by association, Raskolnikov?

    A. By accusing her of being a prostitute
    B. By framing her for the theft of a one-hundred-ruble bill
    C. By accusing her of having an affair with Svidrigailov
    D. By accusing her of abandoning her family

25. Why does Svidrigailov allow Dunya to escape from his apartment after attempting to rape her?

    A. Because she wounds him with a revolver
    B. Because he decides to kill himself
    C. Because he is afraid of Raskolnikov
    D. Because he realizes that she will never love him

ANSWER KEY

1: B; 2: C; 3: A; 4: D; 5: D; 6: A; 7: C; 8: D; 9: B; 10: B; 11: C; 12: B;
13: A; 14: D; 15: B; 16: C; 17: C; 18: A; 19: C; 20: D; 21: C; 22: D;
23: A; 24: B; 25: D

Suggestions for Further Reading

BLOOM, HAROLD, ed. *Fyodor Dostoevsky's* CRIME AND PUNISHMENT. New York: Chelsea House Publishers, reprint edition 2003.

FRANK, JOSEPH. *Dostoevsky.* 5 vols. Princeton, NJ: Princeton University Press, 1979–2003.

GROSSMAN, LEONID PETROVICH. *Dostoevsky: A Biography.* Trans. Mary Mackler. Indianapolis: Bobbs-Merrill Co., 1975.

MAGARSHACK, DAVID. *Dostoevsky.* New York: Harcourt, Brace & World, 1963.

MILLER, ROBIN FEUER, ed. *Critical Essays on Dostoevsky.* Boston: G. K. Hall, 1986.

SEKIRIN, PETER, ed. *The Dostoevsky Archive: Firsthand Accounts of the Novelist from Contemporaries' Memoirs and Rare Periodicals.* Jefferson, NC: McFarland & Co., 1997.

TERRAS, VICTOR. *Reading Dostoevsky.* Madison: University of Wisconsin Press, 1998.

TUTEN, FREDERIC. *Dostoyevsky's* CRIME AND PUNISHMENT. New York: Monarch Press, 1966.

REVIEW & RESOURCES